5 Minutes of sunshine

Letters to a Perfect Child

Thomas Plummer

Illustrated by Jeff Camish

HEALTHY ≡LEARNING™

ISBN: 978-1-60679-306-0

Library of Congress Control Number: 2014940268

Cover design: Jeff Camish
Book layout: Cheery Sugabo
Illustrations: Jeff Camish

Healthy Learning
P.O. Box 1828
Monterey, CA 93942
www.healthylearning.com

Dedication

The universe owed me nothing, but has given me everything. Out there beyond success and money is love, which is the gift we often lose chasing other things that never satisfy or fulfill a life through the years. My life is complete because of the love of three women. I thank you Susan for being the love of my life. Thank you Jillian for being the wonderful daughter I never expected to find. And thank you Madison, the perfect child, whose love inspired this book. Papa loves you Madison, and always will.

Contents

Dedication 3

5 Minutes of Sunshine 7

Dear Madison 15

Friends 21

Making a Difference 27

Respect 33

The Layers of Life 39

What Is a Good Person 49

Your Mother 55

The Magic of Books 65

The Meaning of Money 71

Finding God 81

Madison at Six 87

Money Can't Buy Happiness 93

A Time to Be Still 105

Do What You Say You Will Do 111

Nana 117

Life in Motion 125

Value Your Life 131

Living Within Yourself 137

Nothing Lasts Forever 143

Always Remember Papa Loves You 149

About the Author 159

5 Minutes of sunshine

It was late in the season on Cape Cod, a time when the last of the warm winds that sweep the cape during the glorious, but notoriously short, summers were giving way to the first chilling gusts off of the cold north Atlantic waters surrounding our island. I was sitting on the front steps of the house, the side of our home sheltered from the increasingly colder and steady winds off the ocean. Leaves tumbled down our street, driven by short gusts, and chaotic clouds were racing through at a rapid pace, occasionally revealing short bursts of sunshine that would change a chilly early fall day into a warm and beautiful last touch of summer.

My granddaughter Madison was four at the time. She was running around the yard at a frenetic pace, emitting shrieks of joy and enthusiasm only a small child can generate playing on her own. The day was fading quickly, but there was reluctance on my part to take her inside and end a perfect day of play for her and a memory for me.

The sunshine broke through once again, also refusing to give into the lateness of the afternoon. Madison ran back to the steps, turned, and stood inside my arms, gathering a little warmth as she began to tire. I held her in my arms for only about five minutes, and for the first time all afternoon, she was quiet. Her hair smelled like all things little girl and her hands were lying gently on top of mine folded around her.

Sadness settled in for me as I realized there would be few of these moments in the future. She would grow and an afternoon with Papa would be something that would interest her less and less in the coming years. Ever the person who reflects and guides others to help create lives of meaning, the thought dawned on me that Madison would reach a point in her life where I wouldn't be there any longer for her.

My time with her, and the time I could help her in life, guide her through tough times, love her unconditionally when the world would seem to conspire against her, and just be there for her, was finite, and at some point reasonably soon, I would be nothing more than a photo on a shelf and perhaps a memory of a quiet special day.

My five minutes of sunshine would fade, but the challenge that now confronted me was to find a way to be there for Madison in the future when the lessons I have learned in my own life, and from more than 30 years of coaching others, might help her create the magical life she could live someday—a special life full of adventures, fulfillment, and satisfaction from knowing it was a life well spent.

Time assumes an escalating relevance as you age. When you are young, an event just a few days in the future seems like it takes the biggest part of your young life to arrive. A week away is agony and you count the days by the number of times you have to go to bed before you finally get up in the morning to start your adventure. Time when you are young is endless, adventures are around every corner, and your life stretches out a hundred years in front of you. Fall afternoons spent in the sun are too many to count and will always be there when you are four.

Pass 50 years old in your life and important dates in the future become something to savor with a quiet anticipation, accompanied with the mental swing between hoping it will arrive and not wanting it to at all because arrival means another milestone passed and those milestones become fewer and fewer each year.

Time after 50 is a checklist of things undone, and as you age, everyone reaches the point where you realize there will never be enough time to get it all done. This point may be the most humbling realization for any person in the universe—the point where you finally realize there simply isn't enough time left to finish every dream you previously thought you would get to one day and now you must start prioritizing what is important and what must remain a dream to be someday lost.

Children were never a part of my life's plan. I realized early I was selfish in my own way and wanted to live my dreams, on my terms, without the burden of carrying others, and understanding this part of my soul, I knew I would make a poor father. Having children when I was in my 20s or 30s wasn't necessary to complete my life, or myself, and I worked hard to create a life on my own terms and lived by my own rules.

Reality was tough on this philosophy though and the old saying "If you want to make God laugh, just show him your plans" hit me hard. God corrects, and sometimes, that correction resembles a good old-fashioned ass-kicking. I married young, and after more than 20 years together, we grew apart, as do so many people who get married with little thought or reason in their early 20s as to who they are and what they might want in the course of living lives combined.

The old sage advice that you can't be happy with someone until you are old enough to be happy with yourself was as if it were written directly for me. Remarrying in my 40s brought me a woman who was confident in herself, her life, and her business and who was willing to live with an overage wanderer who viewed life as one great adventure.

And she also brought children. Our daughter Jillian was a teenager at the time and she believed she was right and the rest of the world wrong and that the only way to drive a car is pedal down until you are caught. In other words, Madison's mother was just like every other teenage girl in the world at that time. Our son CJ was just about 12 when we met and he was the gentle child who happily sat up all night in the basement watching cooking shows and yelling "bam" along with his favorite chef. He has gone on to be a chef in his early 20s and had a career focus I could only look on with envy.

There has never been a man more mismatched for a fight than I was. Clueless, inpatient, lost, and just plain stupid are all words that describe my first years as a parent. The battle ceased and the situation improved when I found one piece of advice that changed my outlook. This nugget was in a little editorial in a paper and was written by a man talking about being in the same situation. His advice, which I hungrily acquired, was just become the father you didn't have to be. In other words, just become what you might have been and quit fighting the inevitable. If you love her, he said, then you have to love the kids too or nothing will work. This was a definite "Duh" moment, but it became advice that changed my life once again.

Both kids survived my early attempts at parenthood and Jillian now works for me full time, running my company. Her daughter Madison is now four, and once again, I was thrown into the fight weaponless and clueless as our first grandchild arrived. Teenagers were trouble enough, but bottles, diapers, car seats, and all the other paraphernalia pertinent to small children were inexplicable things way outside my experience base, but again, we all survived and I can now not imagine a life without the children or the world's perfect child, which this comment alone should prove that even someone late to the dance can master the basics of being a proud grandfather.

This little book was written for Madison for those days when she finds herself alone, afraid, confused, or overwhelmed by life and when there isn't anyone close she can talk to who could offer the advice or guidance that might make her day, and her life, easier to understand and ultimately more fulfilled.

This book was also written for the parents who struggle to put into words advice that might make a difference in a child's life. There is a commonality in the lives of many people in their early 20s, and most young people in that age group share many of the concerns, fears, and frustrations that can seem so stressful and so huge at the time. Sadly, very few of these seekers have anyone to turn to who will, or can, offer insight or advice that would ease some of the pain.

Mentoring is hard, and far too many parents are simply too busy and too overwhelmed by their own lives or just not prepared to guide a 20-something person through tough times. The spirit might be willing, but the ability or willingness might not be there and perhaps the biggest block to helping anyone is just having the patience to sit, listen, and offer a path. Many people are so unsure in their own lives that they are hesitant to take a stand or tell someone what to do in his or her life, and most hedge their advice by trying to give a simple, advice-column style of guidance that in reality helps no one solve anything.

The letters here are the result of more than 30 years of listening to an extremely wide variety of people of all ages who were all trying to move forward in their lives. Right or wrong in their search, many of these seekers sought direction and a plan and I was always willing to give one based on who they were and what they wanted to accomplish today and in the years to come.

Most advice starts with a simple concept: You can't get anywhere if you don't know where you are going and my first few letters to my granddaughter are designed to help her constantly keep her life projected into the future. The lesson I most importantly want to teach her is that you cannot have everything you want, but you can have anything you want in your life and reach any goal if you know where you are going and what you want from the experience of being you.

But life is also about the journey itself and the richness you can find by seeking adventure, learning throughout your lifetime, taking risks, and grounding yourself in a spiritual base based on your own exploration. Internal principles you acquire yourself through constantly examining your own life are the only ones that will stick. You can share your principles, or life rules, with others, but nothing becomes yours until you understand what that principle means to you and only then can you internalize it.

The principles and ideas I have found and I am trying to share here were hard fought for in my life, but perhaps the hardest observation as an aging adult is that you just can't be there forever. Seeking balance and creating a life worth living are noble goals, but at some point, it becomes someone else's turn. Through my years of consulting and coaching others, the one hard fact I've learned is that you simply run out of time. Being a realist, I'm okay with not being there in the future, but not being able to help and guide Madison is not acceptable to me; therefore, a book was needed to fill the gap.

And I am sure that somewhere soon there will be a time in my life that I might give most everything I have ever achieved, and everything I have worked for through the years, to have just another five minutes of sunshine with my perfect child.

This book was designed to be a personal book that helps guide readers toward making their own discoveries as to who they are, what they want from life, and how to live a life of value and happiness.

This book was also designed as a journaling book. If you are a parent, you might work on writing down your own key thoughts as to what you want to share with your children in the future—much as was done here for a child that is a long way from understanding the true content and messages contained in this book. As a parent, you have lived a life and learned your own lessons. Use the journal pages here to write your own letters and leave your own thoughts as to the important things you want to pass along to your children inspired by the letters to Madison.

If you are reading this on your own, and for your own life, use the pages at the end of each letter to write about how you think now and where you want to go in the future, then come back to those notes year after year and compare your goals to where you are in your life at that time.

There are also guiding questions at the end of each letter that will help you focus on the important messages contained in each one. These questions are just a starting point and should help you to get your own writing flowing. If you want to get the most out of this little book, write down the important things you have learned that you might want to pass on to your children, write down the issues you are struggling with in your life, and also include the mistakes you have made and what you have learned from them. Your life is unique and what you have to teach others is important.

Your life, your family

_____

_____

_____

_____

_____

_____

_____

_____

_____

_____

_____

_____

_____

_____

_____

_____

_____

_____

_____

_____

_____

Dear Madison

Dear Madison,

Ever since you were a little baby, I have been whispering in your ear that Papa loves you. This little book is an extension of that love and everything you mean to me as my granddaughter.

We played one day a long time ago at our house by the water. The day was chilly and cloudy, but you had energy and insisted that you had to be outside playing in the yard. There was coldness in the air and you wore a dressy long coat and a pair of rubber boots, which when you were four years old were always a part of your wardrobe no matter what time of year it seemed to be.

You were busy that day running from late blooming flower to flower, up and down the steps and leaping off the small stonewall that was in front of our house. You laughed, screamed, giggled and were wonderfully enthralled by your own magic, as I was. Just as the chill was becoming too much and I decided to take you into the house, the sun broke through the clouds instantly warming us.

I will never know what was in your mind, and you were far too young to remember, but you came to me as I was sitting on the steps and stood facing the yard with your head laid back on my shoulder and your small hands on top of mine, which were wrapped around you. You stood quietly for only about five minutes, but those five minutes would make for a perfect lifetime of memories for me.

Time passes at a speed that only accelerates as you age. During those five minutes I realized that I would not be part of your life forever; that sooner or later my time would be gone and you would be in the world without me. No one was outside that day but just you and I, and no one saw my tears that reflected a sense of loss of something I had only then realized I had.

This book is for the days in your life when I am not here. Everything in this book was written personally to you to be read someday when you are probably in your 20s and then later in your life if the letters indeed help answer some of the questions you will undoubtedly face as you begin your own adventure in life.

You will not remember, but I spent most of my life trying to help good young men and women grow in their lives and their businesses. Much of what I did involved almost acting as a parent or mentor and many of the seemingly endless conversations I had with my young protégés in my career involved the big lessons in life. They came to me for business, but I believe most stayed with me for long years because I cared enough to listen and guide them through failures, successes, the moments when they were scared of losing everything and other rough times where life was a struggle that might not be won and where a strong opinion and a lot of life experience mattered most.

The experience of my over 30 years talking about the things that matter, and that lead to a life fulfilled, is what is contained in this book. The letter format makes sense to me since I hope you always remember me talking to you and through the letters I hope I can always be there for you; therefore, this was done as a series of letters on different subjects that to me are timeless and universal in nature. Everyone, Madison, will at times be confused, a little lost in life, scared about work and struggling through all the variety of relationships in your life from parents, to friends, to whomever you choose to love.

When your days are lonely and you search for the answers to some of life's most daunting questions, I hope you get a blanket and a cup of tea as your Nana always did and that she found to be so comforting and pull out Papa's old book and read a little. Perhaps the help you need that day can be found in these pages, but if not there will be always one thing to be found there for sure and it will be clear on every page you read...Papa loves you, Madison, and always will.

18

1. What were the most significant moments in your life and why?

2. What important lessons have you learned in life you would want to share with your children, or with others, in the future?

3. Have you written letters to your children to be read in the future of whom you are now, how you lived and the things you want them to remember of you as the person you are now?

4. What if you are not there in the future? What gifts would you like to leave others about who you were and what you believed? Pictures, letters and thoughts about who you are now should all be compiled and treasured instead of just someday trying to remember the important things that should never be lost.

5. We all grow in life. Spend time writing about who you are now, how you lived, the mistakes you have made and how you want to live in the future. Dreams remain just dreams until you put them into writing.

Your life, your family

Your life, your family

_____

_____

_____

_____

_____

_____

_____

_____

_____

_____

_____

_____

_____

_____

_____

_____

_____

_____

_____

_____

_____

_____

_____

Friends

To my Madison,

When you are young, it seems everyone is your friend and those early friendships made during your school years will be there for you forever, but you will find, my love, that your definition of the experience of friends and what they mean to you, and what even the idea of friendship means, will change as you change and grow throughout your life.

How you acquire and relate to other people in your life will largely be determined by how you choose to live your life. Stay in one place for life and your friendships will be long and often based on people who you meet young and who stay part of your life as you grow older. There are many happy people who grow up, and then grow old, living in the same town they were born in and who surround themselves with the same circle of friends they have maintained since their first days of school. This is a good lifestyle if it appeals to you and it is what you seek from life.

If, on the other hand, you choose to move about often, seeking the experiences of new cities or countries, your friendships will often be based on those experiences, and the more often you move, the more likely you are to continue gathering new circles around you each time, putting more time and distance between you and your earlier friendships. This lifestyle is rewarding in the adventures you will have in life, but you will also realize that it is sometimes painful to lose a circle of new friends each time you move on. There is also richness in this lifestyle, and if you find that this is how you want to live, you must always work hard to maintain the friendships you value as you move again to the next adventure.

As people age, they also come to understand the differences between people who are close to you and people who truly become friends. We call our circle of acquaintances friends and many people use this term loosely, but the true definer of friendship often comes down to who you will trust with your innermost thoughts and secrets.

As you age, you will have many friends in the outer circle of acquaintances, but you will find that true friends become rarer as you progress through life and these are the people who you will want to give your time, energy, and support to keep those friendships and where you will be willing to work hard to keep these friends forever.

Sadly, friends will drift in and out of your life. Families come, jobs change, life moves you elsewhere, and the people you love and trust are now miles away, surrounded by new circumstances and a new set of acquaintances. The most important thing I can teach you about friends is that if you want someone in your life, you should take the lead and dedicate time to keep that person close to you. If you want friends, you have to be a friend and it is your role in any friendship to reach out and keep those friends close to your heart. If the person is worthy of being called your friend, then he or she is worthy of calls, trips, and contact that lets the person know you miss him or her and that you are thinking of him or her at that moment.

Days pass quickly when you are busy in your life and time can pass so fast that you simply lose the ones you love. Refuse to do this, Madison. If you find people you care about and want to keep in your life, reach out to them often and never let go of those you love. And as rare as it is now—and will be even more so in your life—actually talking to someone for even a few minutes is so much more powerful than a few lines of text delivered impersonally through whatever device you have at hand.

An evening with friends, filled with conversation and perhaps a glass of wine and plenty of laughter, is in many ways the essence of life and is something that isn't determined by how much money you have or where you live. Friends are life, Madison, and the good ones are worth effort and whatever it might take to keep them close to your side.

24

1. Who are your closest friends and why are they important to you?

2. What would you like to teach your child about friendship?

3. We sometimes lose friends as we move, age, change jobs, or start a new life. Who did you lose as a good friend and what will you do to find him or her? Why do you miss that friendship?

4. What are the values that make for a good friend?

5. There is an old saying that if you want friends, you have to be a friend. Are you the friend that you want others to be? If you are, what things should a good friend be to others? If not, what do you need to change to make and keep the friends you want in your life?

6. Leave your own letter on friendship for your child.

Your life, your family

Your life, your family

_____

_____

_____

_____

_____

_____

_____

_____

_____

_____

_____

_____

_____

_____

_____

_____

_____

_____

_____

_____

_____

_____

_____

Making a difference

Dear Madison,

There always comes a time, at least for people who are blessed with a mind that questions the meaning of life, where you question the purpose of your own life. Many people intellectually understand the question, but few people take the time and effort to find the answer. Asking "Why am I here and does my life matter?" has probably scared more people into running away and hiding than any other thing you could ask them. But you are here for a purpose, and while the answer may not come to you without a lot of work, just the act of asking why will always force you to live at a higher level than most people achieve.

Too many people wait until they are too old to ask themselves this question. Waiting until you are the age I am now as I write this to you is waiting too long. You want to seek and explore who you are and where you are going early in life and then make this question a part of your constant ability to grow and change.

There is a difference between finding your life's work and finding your purpose in life. What you do for work may change a number of times throughout your working days and I hope you explore many interesting choices and take the risks that come with setting out on a new career path.

It used to be said that your choice of work defines your life, but as I look back at the thousands of people who I helped and coached in my own career, I would say that it is how you choose to do whatever work you are doing at the time that defines the quality of your life. Being engaged in your work, giving it everything you have, and only doing work you find interesting and meaningful is more important than the money you might make or the size of the office you might one day have.

The purpose of this letter, though, is defining why you exist at all—a question that can never really be answered, but one that is always important to how you grow as a person in life. There is an underlying principle that can help ground you in your search, and this tenet states you should exist to make a difference in this world.

Making a difference, or leaving the world a better place because you were here, is what separates a life lived and a life well lived. It is also the key to leaving the world remembered as a person who improved the lives around him or her, rather than just leaving—soon to be forgotten by everyone.

You will encounter many people who exist to merely take what they can get from others. Takers want everyone to serve their needs while giving nothing back that matters. Givers are the people who are willing to help others, improve their communities, follow careers that somehow improve the lives of those around them, and live each day by trying to change the world they touch. It is contradictory in thought, but the takers usually end up with nothing of value in their lives, while the givers end up surrounded by friends, family, and money. Maybe it is the karma thing, or just the humor of a God that rewards people willing to give, but striving to make a difference in the world almost always leads to a life full of abundance and opportunity and rich in family and friends.

My life was built on this premise. It was always more important to me to help someone, even if he or she couldn't pay me today—or maybe ever—just for the good feeling it gave me to help a person who needed guidance or, worse, was down and out in life, but it seemed the more I gave away, the more I received and what came back always exceeded what went out.

Make a difference, Madison. Change the world around you every day. Be that person who gives and asks nothing in return. Do this, and you will end up with more in your life than you could have ever dreamed of, my child.

1. Answer the question for yourself: Why are you here and what are you doing to make a difference in the world?

2. What do you want your life's work to be?

3. What would you like to teach your child about making a difference in life?

4. There are givers and there are takers in life. What do these two terms mean to you?

5. Write a letter to your child about what it takes to make a difference in the world. When did you know your purpose? How did you find it in life? What mistakes did you make during your early life and search?

Your life, your family

Your life, your family

_____
_____
_____
_____
_____
_____
_____
_____
_____
_____
_____
_____
_____
_____
_____
_____
_____
_____
_____
_____

Respect

Dearest Madison,

There was always one rule that served me well throughout my adult life when it came to living in a world with so many different types of people and so many people who come in and out of your life every day. Finding your own place in the world is not easy for people, and many people—and sadly, too many women—are often dominated by someone else's power or personal agenda. Finding your place, and keeping your personal perspective when it comes to dealing with others, will be hard and you'll find many people will try to bend you to their will by their influence, power, money, and/or personality.

Struggling to develop a style adaptation for every person will not work, and while you should learn to judge everyone by his or her actions and not what he or she does for a living or his or her current circumstances, you might find it hard to constantly check your premises for each and everyone you encounter. People make money, lose money, sometimes choose careers that keep their lives simple, and often just have tough times in their lives. What doesn't change for any of these people is who they are at the core. Good people are simply good people, and no matter what the circumstances in their lives are, they remain loyal to doing the right things in life without hurting or damaging others.

My rule for living with other people is simple: Show respect for everyone, but be intimidated by no one.

If you have a personal relationship, it is sometimes easy to lose your personality and own belief system to someone who tries to change you. This rule will help you keep the proper perspective based on the fact that you are a valuable individual, and while you may seek to live with someone special, or work for someone who seems to have the power of money or personality, you should never let anyone, under any circumstances, nor for any reason, intimidate you.

This rule applies to work, friends, to the kid at the coffee shop counter, the president of the company where you work, and the waitress who serves you today and who made little money for such hard work,; this woman deserves your respect as a human being, as does every other person you will meet throughout your journey.

People who forget this rule often feel they are better than others and that being belligerent or mean to someone gives them a sense of power over another. Money and power don't make you a better person, and if you achieve these things in your life, remember that there are others less fortunate in life who deserve your kindness and respect until they do something that negates that for you. There is simply no reason in the world to be mean and disrespectful to anyone doing honest work and trying to live life as best he or she can, and there is definitely no reason anyone who flaunts power or money should ever feel superior over just having a few more dollars in his or her bank account than you do.

Give your respect freely to everyone, but always remember someone may have more money, or more things, or might be further along in life, but that person has no right ever to intimidate or hurt you in any way. Money often leads to arrogance for too many, and you will always find the fool using the power of money to hurt others. When it is your turn, Madison, always remember the rule works both ways. There will always be those who have more than you, and there will always be those who have less, but it shouldn't matter to you either way—everyone deserves respect. Never forget, however, that you must not live your precious life being intimidated by anyone.

1. Have you struggled in the past with a bully or someone who tried to dominate your life with his or her power? What lesson did you learn from this experience and what would you like to share with your child in the future?

2. How does one show respect for others? What could you teach others about this?

3. Who has earned your respect and, most importantly, why? What does respect mean to you and how do you define it to others?

4. Write a letter to your child in the future about how you feel about respect and how you should treat others.

Your life, your family

Your life, your family

_____

_____

_____

_____

_____

_____

_____

_____

_____

_____

_____

_____

_____

_____

_____

_____

_____

_____

_____

_____

_____

The layers
of life

Dear Madison,

You will find times where you need advice in your life, and as I have said to you in all these letters, I hope this book will be one source to turn to through the years as you grow and experience life's many adventures.

My strongest motivation in writing this book is that I also firmly believe you will find few people in your life who are older than you who are willing, or able, to give you help and guidance. As a seeker, meaning one who spends his or her life looking for the answers to life's many riddles, this might frustrate you as it has me through the years, but there is a legitimate reason many older people in your life will not be able to give you any valid answers concerning the problems you will face.

The primary reason the older generation may not seem willing to help is that much of their experience is generational and simply won't apply to what you face. Having someone tell you how a job or relationship should be handled today based on an experience that is 40 years old usually doesn't work well. The culture of 40 years ago was different and how people thought and acted in society, and personally, was far removed from what you will experience as an adult woman in your time and within your generation.

Yes, there are consistencies that must be maintained in life, such as how you treat others, or the personal ethics you must always maintain. Hurting others, not living up to your personal word, personal responsibility for your actions, and developing a strong work ethic are examples of ideas that transfer well from generation to generation and should be honored. But there are other ideas that don't transfer from one generation to another, such as views on marriage, discrimination as to sex or race, or how women should be treated today versus how they have been treated by older generations.

My unique experience—of being older but working with so many hundreds of younger people through so many years as a personal mentor and coach—gave me an advantage when it came to guiding another generation—an advantage few other people can lay claim to in their lives. My thoughts had to constantly evolve so I would always be able to help those who needed guidance and direction, but I was also always the one who fought to understand the difference between those things I hold sacred, such as no discrimination, and those ideas that are transient and need to evolve or be eliminated in my life.

Perhaps the strongest representation of the difference between those in your generation and the generations that make up the older people in your life, such as all of your grandparents, is how you will mature through your chosen work. How your grandparents, or even your parents, approached work and careers is different from how I expect your generation will seek to live and work.

Back in the day of your grandparents, our lives were culturally determined in many ways and everyone passed through most of the same layers of life. You went to high school, or if you were one of the lucky few, you went off to college, you left school, and then you started on your chosen career. This career was often your life's work—whether you wished it to be or not—and you would usually stay with this career until you retired in your mid-50s and then you spent your alleged golden years waiting to die, which usually happened about six years or so after retirement.

There were exceptions to this rule of course. There were many people from this generation who would drift from job to job—always with the thought that the next one would be the big one where the big money or big opportunity came. Most of these people were eventually disappointed by each choice, but few of them realized that there were no perfect jobs that would save them and that the failure they endured in each choice they made was their own fault, not the fault of their current boss or company.

There were also many people from that era who would survive retirement, but over time, the brave individuals who would think deeply about such things realized retiring so young was senseless and living a life where you were active, involved, and useful was far more important than how much golf you could play, lawns you could cut, or shopping you could do.

The layers of life will be different for you and I expect that even what I have written here might change for people your age, but the options you will have in your life are far greater than those who love you and who have gone before you. Having even a simple model to think about might help your journey and help you understand that what worked for generations ago may not work for you, leaving you to discover your own paths in life.

Remember, no one has to experience these in any set order, and you might be the person who finds your own way in life by skipping a layer—something that is somewhat of a family tradition—but knowing these layers are out there and part of a typical person's life experience will hopefully help you make better decisions for yourself.

- *Your 20s:* This should be the time period where you explore your passion and try on lots of different jobs, experiences, and relationships. There is no need to decide too early what you want to do with your life, and the more of life's experiences you have in your 20s, the easier it will be later to create a life based on doing what you are truly passionate about. Read, try different types of work, travel as much as you can, maybe live in a few big cities, but most importantly, take chances and try things. The only failure you should ever think about at this stage of your life is not that you tried something and didn't like it, but that you were too scared to try something new at all.

- *Your 30s:* This should be the time in your life where you declare your passion and begin to create a career based on doing what you love. Dedicate yourself to being the best at what you choose. Perhaps the best advice I ever received was to learn more about one thing than anyone else and you will never be poor or out of work. It was good advice then, and I think it still will be when you read this for yourself someday. Find your one thing, my perfect child, and then commit to being the best at it you can be.

- *Your 40s:* This is the decade of your life where you become the master of what you choose to do. These is the age where you now have the experience and maturity to take the passion from your earlier years and start to create wealth, with the goal of becoming that expert or master at something you love. The maturity of these years allows you to fully grasp the depth of your work and your life. It is a sad fact, however, that many people who don't identify their passion by these years will often struggle for the rest of their lives. You don't want to be the person still looking for something meaningful to do, and still blaming others for your failure, when you are in your 40s. Commit to your passion and commit to the quality of life you create for yourself.

- *Your 50s:* These should be your wealth-building years, although you might find that this can happen at any time in your life when you are working hard on your dreams. There will be many people in their 20s who create wealth through the delivery of a good idea, and there will also be others who will find it later through the long, slow process of experience and maturity. Either way is right, as long as it is your way. These are also the years where your actions and the way you live will determine the quality of the rest of your life. Each decade should lead to a bigger goal—and that goal is to live healthy by making choices that ensure no matter how many years you live, you will always live as an active participant in life and not as someone regulated to watch life slip away due to bad choices. Eat healthy, exercise every day of your life, avoid the thieves of life, such as drugs and smoking, and build yourself into a person who just gets better with age rather than one who fades away decades earlier than he or she should have from not being smart enough to take care of yourself.

- *Your 60s:* These are the years where you should be guiding others and paying back the universe for the success you have achieved. The most important way to do this is by helping others through your money and through giving your time. Pay back, Madison, for all you will be given, and share your good fortune always with others. This is also a time where you enjoy the achievements of your life, and I hope you have a significant person in your life at this stage to enjoy that glass of wine (or the perfect hike, ski day, or trip, or just a simple, quiet day at the beach) with.

- *Your 70s:* This is when you start life all over again. This is the age where you can do those crazy things you didn't get to earlier. Remember, you can't have everything you want in life, but you can have anything you want. Some experiences or goals in life will have to be set aside to accomplish the ones you want most, but later, you can revisit these other not-yet-forgotten passions that were slightly less important at the time compared to your big dreams. Your 70s can be the years where you live the great adventure, write the book you always wanted, take guitar lessons, learn to play a sport, or just pack up everything and ride the trains of Europe. Life is not over when you are 70; it's just a time in your life of rejuvenation and another start on the next adventure. Remember again that the quality of your life will be determined by the quality of your health and wellness. How you eat, live, and work out when you are younger lays the foundation for the quality of your years later. You can be 70 and be 90 physically and mentally or you can be 70 and be 50 forever in your body and spirit if you take care of yourself. Choose life, Madison, and choose to get more life out of your years for as long as you can.

I think I should talk about finding your passion one more time. All finding your passion means, my child, is find something that is important to you, something that has the potential to keep you in money during your life, and something that keeps you from being trapped doing work that is meaningless or boring. Passion is finding something you want to willingly give your undivided attention every day and that the hours spent involved with what you love seem to be the best hours of your life. I found this in my own life through writing, reading, and fitness and through my love of business as a way to keep myself fed.

When I wrote this, I had been doing the same work as a business consultant and coach for 37 years, and I can say I never worked a day in my life. Every day, I was able to get up and do what I wanted and help someone who needed my guidance and direction, and through these things, I was able to make enough money to do the things important to me without ever being dependent on anyone else financially.

I hope you find this passion for something in your own life, and I hope you always find a way to live within yourself. The one true gift I hope to leave you, my child, is permission to be wonderful in your own way no matter what you choose to do.

46

1. Where do you feel you are in life now? Are you settled and committed to your passion, or are you still seeking?

2. What are you passionate about and why aren't you making that your life's work?

3. Where do you see yourself in five years?

4. What thoughts and emotions about the stages of life do you have now and that you would like to share with your child in the future?

5. Have you ever worked doing something you didn't like? How did that feel and what did you learn from that experience?

6. Write a letter to your child in the future as to what you have learned about the layers in life.

Your life, your family

Your life, your family

_____
_____
_____
_____
_____
_____
_____
_____
_____
_____
_____
_____
_____
_____
_____
_____
_____
_____
_____
_____
_____

What is a good person

Dear Madison,

One of the constant themes in everything I will write for you is that you must learn how to live life on your own terms.

In the era I grew up in, being part of some large company, being part of a team (which meant nothing more than doing what the boss wanted you to do), being someone who lived conservatively and avoided risk, was the cultural norm of the times. We even had a saying in that era where the tallest nail was pounded first, which was just another way of saying if you stood out from the group, you would be the first one to be humbled or corrected.

This thankfully began to change around the time you were born and the new generation of workers and thought producers were those willing to take chances, willing to fail and fail often, and willing to create their own lives and their own paths based on the passions in their lives that they wished to follow.

I think I was secretly always one of those people in that I tried the corporate world and found its severe structure too restrictive for my chosen life, leading me to revolt and overreact, which turned out to be a good thing. This led to my spending my entire life doing exactly what I pleased: Chasing the things that excited me and being unafraid of failure, but never afraid of making money or being able to take care of myself.

Being a good person means that once you recognize who you are and what you want—understanding this certainty might change and evolve over the years—you stay true to that passion and then live your life to a personal standard that allows you to maintain your personal respect and the respect of those around you. Being a good person also means you set higher standards for yourself than others, and you live by those standards without ever compromising them.

It does not matter how other people chose to live. There will be friends, and even those closer to you, who will cheat on spouses, cheat friends for money, and lie to gain an advantage or be willing to hurt someone else for some type of personal advantage. There will also be people who lose everything of value in their lives due to drugs or alcohol and you will even find those who lose the quality of their life by simply eating themselves to death. Most pain in the world is self-inflicted and most of the people who suffer around you often brought that suffering on themselves, but then chose to blame others for their failings rather than accept personal responsibility.

You will make mistakes, and those are part of life, but I can tell you after a long and interesting life that giving up your standards for a short-term gain is not worth the damage it will do to your soul and to your self-esteem. It is funny to say, but perhaps the highest standard you can set is setting high standards. Few people understand what true personal responsibility is or means, but you cannot be a good person without understanding and accepting that idea as your own.

When you were young, I spent most of my life at the time helping young businesspeople, who were passionate about a life in fitness, find their way. The talks and consulting would always start with business, but almost all these long talks led to deep discussions on life and how to live it well. My advice then, and it would be the same now if I were sitting with you in your 20s and helping you discover yourself as I helped all those other young seekers, is being a good person is merely defining your personal values and then living within those values and never compromising who you are or what you believe.

My advice is to first set a moral standard representing your personal worth. This standard is built on personal respect. Do you respect your mind by constantly trying to improve it? Do you respect your body by seeking health and avoiding putting anything in your body that will cause harm? Do you respect your personal boundaries by being selective with whom you might choose to sleep with in the future and the type of work you are willing to do, and by being unwilling to sell your values for money or for short-term gain? Are you willing to help someone who truly can't help him or herself as opposed to helping those who refuse to take any responsibility for who they are and how they live?

Personal responsibility is the key to being a good person. Always do what you promise. Always be there for a friend. Always value yourself and your body over everything else. Always seek the experience and live as a full participant in life, not as an observer of life. Understand and respect money as a simple tool that allows you to live life on your own terms.

Blame no one else for mistakes you make. Be honest and be willing to sacrifice anything else before you lose that value. Hurt no one. Respect everyone, but be intimidated by no one. Seek God on your own terms and on your own path, but spend time looking. Seek the counsel of others, but always make your own decisions at the end as to what is best for you, what allows you to retain your values, and what will bring you the greatest gain and peace in your life.

It is your life, Madison, and someday in your future, when you look back on that life, only you can answer if you were a good person or not because only you will know in your heart if you lived by your own values and to a higher standard you set for yourself.

1. What does living life on your own terms mean to you?

2. What are the important things you believe in that define who you are and how you want to live?

3. What are your personal values? How would you define those to your child in the future?

4. What does being a good person mean to you? What would you teach someone else about being a good person?

5. How would you like your child to turn out in the future? What values would you like him or her to have? Write a letter to your child defining what it means to be a good person and how you hope your child lives in the world as he or she grows into an adult.

Your life, your family

Your Mother

For my lovely Madison,

As a person gets older, his or her perception of what his or her mother was like will change as he or she idealizes remembrances and the past slowly fades and is often mentally rewritten. We often mentally change or modify the memories of our childhood into something warm and fuzzy everyone refers to as mostly happy childhood days, or you sometimes tend to live in sadness as an adult, lamenting a lost childhood that might have been filled with pain, insecurity, or a lack of a caring and loving family to nurture and protect you.

People who have had hard pasts, burdened by dysfunctional mothers and fathers who robbed their children of their happy younger years due to bitter divorces, personal addictions, or other nightmares adults inflict on their families, often either cling to that harshness as a badge of honor, or simply get past it and move on to better days ahead. How your past affects you is always your choice as an adult, but this judgment is set on course by those around you at the time who loved you and protected you. Never be a victim, my child, and always seek the goodness that can be found in almost every situation.

Your childhood had many of the typical childhood traumas, including a divorce between your parents, the addition of a stepfather, who proved to love you as much as his own children, and all the rigors and nonsense that comes from being part of a newly formed extended family. Your childhood was much better than most and everyone in your life banded together to make sure that despite the changes that were happening to the adults, you were always safe and loved. The one constant, however, always there for you through all the changes in your younger life, was the love of your mother.

Children view and judge their mothers differently at different times in their lives. This happens because the lens we use to look back at the past changes as we age and what we think we remember changes over time as we age and mature. The experience of your life changes you and this changes how you view your mother and others in your life over time.

Much of this ever-changing perception of who your mother was at different times in your life is based on two simple ideas. First of all, your mother, as all women experience, was in a constant stage of personal change as she aged and matured in life and in her career. Secondly, you will remember who she was at the time differently, at different times in your life, as you age and mature as a woman. For example, you will eventually understand and respect many of the rules and beliefs offered by your mother then that drive you and so many other young women into wanting to leave home when you are 17, but later, those same things that infuriate every blooming and flowering young woman will become part of your guidance for your own children someday.

Many women never get a chance to know their younger mother as a woman in her prime years with a life outside of just being a mother. Besides the occasional video or picture, you were simply too young to appreciate and understand who your mother was when you are still only six or younger.

This letter is about your mother and who she was when this was written and when you were still flashing fingers to show your age, but it is also about who she was to me, and why I love her as much as I do.

Your Nana and I didn't end up with each other until we were older adults, which we laughingly credit as to why our relationship worked. Even when you were in your preschool days, so many of the other kids were already products of extended families—something the kids took as the new normal while the parents still were attempting to juggle relationships between two sets of parents, added kids, new grandparents, and the occasional crazy relative every family seems to have, but only discusses after a few glasses of wine. Extended families and all the combinations make for interesting lives and the children often seem to adapt to their new lives far easier than the adults.

Nana and I were strong-willed people in our early days who attempted to make the world as we wanted it to be, and only when that drive faded in our careers were we able to find and value each other. There were never kids in my life, as I chose to avoid them in my early years. There were always too many adventures, too many trips, and so much that I wanted from life that I just didn't want or need children. Perhaps I was too selfish to have kids, and I knew early in my life that I would not have been a good father in those younger years.

And then came your mother. Marrying Nana was a package deal, meaning your mother and your uncle were included as part of the marriage. In other words, I went from no children to teenagers, and if there was ever someone not ready for that party, it was your Papa.

There aren't enough books or support groups out there to prepare someone who laughed at the restrictions others endured with children, cringed at the endless baby pictures, and thought the only good child was a child asleep to becoming an overnight parent of teenagers. If nothing else, this proved that God does indeed have a weird sense of humor. But in many ways, this newest adventure in my life turned out to be the best, especially as your mother and I eventually grew into becoming father and daughter. It took you and your mother to convince me that there still might be hope for a secondhand parent and grandparent.

Your mother was never close to her father after she left the house in her early teen years. Someday, the two of them might make peace with each other, and perhaps by the time you can read and understand this, they have, and I always believed they should try again someday, but because of this estranged relationship, the opportunity was there for me to practice my newly acquired parenting skills. That is the sad by-product of so many extended families: It always seems that a parent is lost in the shuffle and it takes a strong child and a persistent, loving parent to hold his or her place in the child's heart.

As I plunged into the new family, the word disaster comes to mind and it seemed that I never had the answer to the problem at hand, if indeed I understood the problem at all. Slowly, though, your mother and I grew together, and if there were a way to choose any woman on the planet to be my daughter, the choice would still be your mother. It took me many years before I could say "frustrating," "uncommunicative," "pain in the ass," and "I love her as no other daughter" all in the same sentence and mean it.

The words *complicated* and *Jillian* were often used in the same sentence when it came to describing your mother during the first years we were together. Some people learn things in life by asking questions and listening to the answers of those that have gone before them. Others, especially when they are young, only seem to learn life's hard lessons by taking a hard mental beating in the process.

Your mother, in her teenager years and early 20s, was the proud queen of the second category. While we often thought this method of learning was unique to your mother, it seems that culturally, many young women of that era bloomed late. This combination of woman/child, where you were older chronologically but still a struggling teenager in so many other ways, led to a generation of women who always struggled to find a personal identity. This would have been especially hard for a woman of this group to have a child when the woman herself was still not much more than a late-developing young woman.

As to your mother, there was never a situation where she didn't have to do it the hard way despite the advice given, mostly unsolicited, and eventually Nana and I just closed our eyes and hoped she would survive intact. This isn't, by the way, good parenting, but it is a good example of self-preservation by parents and this might be a skill you will need for your own children someday, especially if they follow the same path all the women in your family have since your great-great-grandmother Cora.

Then, one day—magically it seemed—your mother became someone wonderful: still complicated, but also wonderful. Becoming a woman and leaving the young girl you once were behind is a long and arduous process. Your mother evolved as a woman of substance in her late 20s, about the time I was writing these letters to you. She grew as a mother, as a wife, and as a woman who began to find her self-confidence, which confidence in who you are is in many ways what defines us all as fully functioning adults.

Your mother is an intelligent woman, taking after Nana, but until later in her life, she never believed in herself and her abilities. Being intelligent and having faith in who you are and what you can do don't always go together. Some people call this the first step in self-actualization, but others might just call it growing up and maturing. No matter how you label the process, that result in your mother was quite thrilling and wonderful to watch.

You probably remember spending a lot of time in our offices when you were around six years old. You even had your own computer and office, which I might add was spoiling you, but you were as always the perfect child (this is a Papa literary license) and that made you happy, and kept you out of everyone's way, so it was your place to be. Your mother started working for my company when she was barely 20 after briefly working for your Nana.

There was a popular saying back in the day that the apple never falls far from the tree. Your mother and grandmother were so alike that, at times, they drove each other into temporary madness, and working together with Nana when your mother was just 20 wasn't going to be a situation that either one of them would survive for any period of time.

Every woman wants to prove her own worth, possibly as a mother, as a wife, through sports or a career, or maybe in business. Nana always had the drive and was able to live her business dream in an era where many women wouldn't have even tried to do their own company. Your mother grew up in another age where women were finally becoming equals in the workforce and the spirit that made your Nana so successful was also what made your mother so frustrated trying to change the business. One held on to her independence, while the other desperately wanted to establish hers.

Both were bright, creative, and, in their own way, driven women, but both were also somewhat obsessive in that no matter what the situation, either one would show you the way to do it, and if you didn't care to play that way, you might be set outside the door with the dogs. (Keep remembering the "complicated" part about your mother, and Nana too.) This is what also made them special in the universe and why Nana was a successful businesswoman and why your mother was rapidly becoming one. The saying was the apple didn't fall far from the tree, but it always really seemed that when it came to these two, there was just too much energy to put in one business together. Each had to find her own path and do it her own way, which you will also discover about yourself someday.

There was an opportunity in my company where I had to make a difficult decision about someone who had been with me for years. Letting this person go was hard, but the final decision was based on my belief that your mother could step up and rise to the occasion.

She went from phone girl to running the company in a very short period of time and this might have been one of the better decisions I ever made in business. She needed a vehicle to shine in her own light—something that can free so many other women, but so often, their chance never arrives—and she found it in our business. Remember that you should never wait for someone to give you a chance. You will be an intelligent woman and you need to constantly prepare yourself to create your own life and your own opportunities.

There are so many things to remember about your mother in that time of her life. She loved you more that any child could be loved. She screamed loudly riding a zip line, but then wanted to do it again immediately. She read several books a week, just like Nana, and was growing into her intelligence. She was a tall, beautiful woman who sometimes wore funky clothes, short skirts, and tall boots and danced with the love of her life. She could go from an exquisite pain in the ass in one moment to a loving child just seconds later. She set standards high and could become angry if someone failed to meet those expectations, but she also made friends and loved people in a special way. She was beautifully complicated, Madison, just as your Nana was, and just as you will be—the youngest apple to fall from that special tree.

1. What do you remember about your mother as you were growing up? What would you like your child to know about her?

2. What would you like your child to know and remember about your "younger version"?

3. Was your life difficult as a child? What lessons would you like to pass on to your children about living in a difficult situation?

4. Were you the difficult child at some point yourself? Why? What did you learn from that experience of yourself that might help your children someday?

5. Write a letter to your children in the future as to who you are today. Include pictures and create a vision of who you are and how you lived so they may know you as the younger person you once were.

Your life, your family

Your life, your family

The magic
of books

Dear Madison,

Books are magical, or at least they have been in my life. It is probably easy for you to tell how I really feel about books because I wrote one just for you to read when you become a young woman. If you love books enough to write them for those you love, then you understand what is magical in books and this passion is something you want to pass on to others you love.

When I was young, I would often escape to my room and spend entire afternoons reading adventure books, history, biographies, and anything else that could be checked out of the school library, or stolen from the occasional adult in my life who read and who would loan a 12-year-old boy books intended for adults.

Since that early love affair with a soft chair and a good book, and I can still remember a particular oversized anthology of the Old West I eventually wore out due to too much rereading and eventually had to let it go as you would saying goodbye to an old friend, I have never been without being surrounded by books. Books can give peace and the mere sight of a shelf of books, some read and others waiting patiently, can change a stressful day into a quiet, healing moment. The time sitting in a big chair in front of a fireplace that becomes a few lost hours of a special time that is all yours can wipe even the nastiest day out of your mind.

Boxes of books have traveled to every new house I have ever lived in and no house was ever complete without the books being carefully unboxed and put on the shelf. Once the books were at home, I was at home and you could never call a place home without the comfort of having a few of your favorite friends stacked somewhere close.

Your Nana was perhaps one of the fastest readers I have ever seen and it was not unusual for her to read several books a week. Reading was her retreat and her way of shifting from a business mind to a quiet mind, and in all my years with her, I do not remember a single day that she didn't read for at least a few minutes just before bed or sitting in a big chair in front of a window or fireplace.

It is said books provide many of the answers to life and this is true. Good writing forces you to think, question, and grow and even books written just for the sake of escape often add a new thought or insight, allowing you to view life from a different perspective. Much of the experience of life has been written about, and written about well, by authors all around the world and the combination of reading and learning from them, along with acquiring your personal experiences, will lead to a life well lived and fulfilled.

Books, in many ways, have always represented something bigger to me than just reading for the sake of escape or the search for immediate education on some subject I was pursing at the time. My type of reading was often of "follow the thread," meaning that if some subject caught my attention, I would read every related book or reference the author noted I could find, and often, one book would turn into buying 12 more and I could never rest until I followed the thread to the point of understanding.

The point here is that books are not merely for today, but represent the power of pursuing a lifelong addiction to learning. Age diminishes this for many people and you will find many of your classmates from your high school years will have read their last book the day they left the school parking lot, but for others, such as Nana, your mother, and me, books represent some of the best time in our lives and I will probably die curled up with a book in my hand if God smiles on me that day. Reading represents growth and reading forever represents a love for learning and a love for continuing to always seek a mind fulfilled and a mind continually challenged by new thoughts and ideas.

Read, my child. Read to your children and I hope you read someday to your children's children. What you read will be your passion and how you read it might be from a device not yet invented that in no way resembles a book, but read and make reading a part of your life, and someday, you might find the love of books as empowering as we have.

1. What are your favorite books? Why?

2. What book should your child definitely read someday as an adult?

3. Will you read to your children someday? What books would you like to read to them?

4. What other things in life can give you the same feeling of comfort as books?

5. Write a letter to your children about learning and about life.

Your life, your family

Your life, your family

The meaning of money

PLEASE SUPPORT THE ARTS

My dearest granddaughter,

Money is a tool that provides safety and comfort for some people, and is something that is never understood and will remain a source of eternal frustration for others for their entire life. The difference between these opinions, and your personal understanding and relationship with money, is rooted in how you think about what money is and how it works. Your feelings about money will also change as you age, gain education, start a family, perhaps start your own business, or simply try to live each day. Learn this first about money: You don't need huge amounts to achieve happiness, but you need enough to chase your dreams.

From my experience as a person who grew up poor and later became successful in business, money is a tool few people can discuss without elevating themselves to a high level of emotion, and while so much is written about money, there are relatively few people who will ever be in your life who will be able to guide you and teach you about what money does and how it works.

Money was something our family had very little of when I was a child, and the lack of money prevented my mother from living life as she would have dreamed of and from chasing her own passions. When you don't have much, everything goes into keeping the family going and this is how my mother lived for most of her early life, which didn't leave much for doing what she wanted or needed in her life. As with most mothers, the needs of the family outweigh the needs of one's self. Despite this obvious stressful issue in our family that caused so much pain and anxiety for all of us through those years, I never had a formal discussion about money with anyone until I was out of college and on my own.

You will find that the people who understand money the least will be the ones who gather so little of it and those who seek knowledge about how money works in the world will most likely be the ones in your life who will accumulate money over time. What is confusing to many people is that those who have little money are also the ones who have the strongest opinions about it. You will often find that this group's rigid viewpoints are usually obvious excuses to explain why they have never achieved financial success of any kind. Always remember that money is not the most important thing in the world … until you don't have any when you most need it, and at that point, you realize money is a valuable tool that enables you to meet the most basic obligations of your life and beyond.

Money is not really hard to make and almost anyone with a little creativity, and who is willing to get up and go to work, can earn money, and in fact, most people will consistently make money in their lives, but the skill and the art is learning how to accumulate it.

There are a lot of misconceptions about money you will have to deal with throughout your life, and all these misconceptions stem from people who badly manage what they earn or who underearn based on the talents they possess. These cultural fallacies and false assumptions become reality for many people, and if you are not careful, you can become trapped into believing things that may damage you and your family for years.

First of all, money is not evil, as many poorer people declare it to be, although you will also hear this often shouted by young idealistic people who have yet to create anything or who have not yet started their life's journey beyond being a student. Money that you earn yourself through your own hard work, or by your own intellect, is something to be proud of in your life and represents a personal achievement that will set you apart from so many others.

The "money is evil" thought often comes from the belief that people who make money have done so by exploiting others or who have somehow gained what they have in an unfair method. Many of the wealthiest people in the world have made their fortunes honestly by their dedication to what they have created and the pursuit of businesses that represent their personal passions.

These people are the ones who create jobs and wealth for others and who are also the ones who give so much back to help others through charities and donations. These people are the drivers of the world and what they create allows others to live better lives. There are, of course, people in the world who have made money by hurting others, but they are few in reality and pale in comparison to those who have spent their lives chasing their own dreams and carrying along the thousands who benefit and profit from their efforts.

Money to me, once I was old enough to ask questions of those who had been successful, and once I matured enough to understand how money works, only had one purpose … and that purpose is freedom. Simply put, money is freedom and allows you to live life on your own terms.

People who are bad with money often spend their lives under the control of others. These people become trapped in jobs they hate, working for people they don't respect or doing work that devalues them. Without money, these people can't move, change jobs, or seek something better because they live payday to payday and never acquire enough in their lives to give them the freedom to make their own decisions.

Living life on your own terms is the greatest achievement you will ever reach. You do not have to be rich to experience this, but you do have to reach a sophisticated enough level with money where you can live within your own means while always being able to create enough money in your life to keep those dreams going.

Money used to mean the accumulation of "things" and many people who are weak with money use it to buy temporary happiness. Feel bad about yourself, have a bad day at work or in your relationship, and then go spend money you haven't yet earned. This will buy a few minutes of happiness for some people, but over time, living this way just leads to greater debt and a deeper trap that you will have to at some point escape from if you want to achieve true peace in your life.

The culture in our country started to change for the better when you were just a little girl. People started to think of money not as a tool to accumulate more stuff that eventually fails to deliver any type of true happiness, but as a way to gain experiences in their lives. For example, someone who might buy a new car every few years became a person who would drive his or her car for a few years longer and then take the money saved and go on a vacation of a lifetime, go back to school, experience a few months off from a job, try a new career, or acquire a new skill or life adventure that would live in his or her head forever.

This style has always been part of my belief system. I always believed you could make money and still seek a lifestyle based on adventures and living life within your own rules. The businesses I have owned, and the way I have led my life, were always designed to allow me to move where I wanted, take winters off and ski, take days off and ride my bike or play golf, and, in other words, do it my way without the restraints of a boss or someone else who controlled my choices.

One of the most important things I could teach you here is that you should seek a way to make a living that allows you to chase your passion in your work, but also allows you to live a full, creative life now and not wait for some mythical time in the future when you might retire to realize your dreams and then be too old to enjoy the adventures that define your life.

You might find, as your grandmother and I did, that creating your own business is the avenue to deliver your freedom. Creating your own dream, building something of value, and then watching it grow and prosper is one of the more satisfying things a human can do in life—but only if it is your dream and only if starting a business becomes something important to you. The alternative to starting your own business would be to find a career that motivates you and you might find your passion as a schoolteacher, a nurse, a doctor, or as the president of a huge technology company. You can be almost anything you can imagine if you want it badly enough, but always make sure you are living and chasing your dream and no one else's.

There will also always be those who feel that you have to give your money away to help those who never succeeded in their own lives. Some people will deserve your help financially, and you will find that special charity or cause that will speak to your heart and that you might help support through your efforts. Pick carefully and be willing to help those who truly need the help, but be reluctant to help those who are unwilling to stand up and attempt to take care of themselves. Since the beginning of time, there have always been people who don't deserve your help because they fail to help themselves, but are more than willing to live and take from those who have gentle hearts.

There is another old saying that applies here too: You can help a lot more people, and change a lot more lives, with a million dollars in the bank than you can with $100. This also applies to those who feel money is something evil and that people with money don't, or won't, help those in need. Make your money, but share it carefully and only with those who need your help, but do share what you create because it becomes your duty once you make money to help those who can't help themselves.

But there are always going to be too many people who want to live off your efforts and the efforts of those who have the willingness to work hard and the mind and creativity to achieve wealth. Beware of those people. I have always enjoyed helping people who have needed the help, and can't help themselves through the tough times in their lives, but I have avoided those who feel they are entitled to your money simply because they are not willing to do the work it takes to obtain success. Help people and make helping a part of your life forever, but remember that wanting is not the same as needing and pick carefully who you help and why.

So, how do you accumulate money? Many people who work for others can save large amounts of money, giving them the freedom to do the work they love and live where they want, by learning to live within their means. There are literally thousands of books written on this, but every one of them can be reduced to this simple thought: Spend less than you earn. In other words, learn to save a certain percentage of what you make each time you get paid and put it away with the thought that once it is saved, it stays saved forever. Of course, you will at times use this money to take a few months off to go explore Europe or to go back to school or whatever else becomes your dreams and passions, but saving with the thought of never spending is a powerful mind-set that will serve you well.

There is no magic formula for saving money, but the old adage is that if it doesn't hurt, then it isn't enough. Saving about 25 percent of what you make first, before any other bills are paid, would take care of you forever and it is the place to start your thoughts when you get those first checks. Yes, I know the mall is calling, but save the 25 percent first and then enjoy the rest.

Finally, most people are lazy about money and end up trusting people who will take what you have earned and ruin what you have achieved. You must, and the word must is emphasized here, learn enough about money so you never fall prey to those who look for the lazy, the stupid, and the inept who earn money, but have never learned how to invest it or keep it. Spend some serious time learning, ask questions of those who have made and kept their money, and only trust people with your money who are proven to be good at protecting what you have earned.

Remember, no matter what you hear over the years, money only has one purpose and that purpose, again, is to gain the power to live life on your own terms by achieving a freedom to take risks, do only the work that makes you happy, and live where you want and when you want.

1. What have you learned about money so far in your life? What would you like to teach others about money and work from what you have learned?

2. What does "Money is freedom" mean to you?

3. What does "Living life on your own terms" mean to you?

4. Everyone makes mistakes with money. What would you like to teach others about the mistakes you have made in the past with money?

5. Are you a good saver of money? If yes, how do you do it? If not, what mistakes do you make with money you could share with others?

6. Write a letter to your children in the future about money and what they can learn from your life.

Your life, your family

Your life, your family

_____
_____
_____
_____
_____
_____
_____
_____
_____
_____
_____
_____
_____
_____
_____
_____
_____
_____
_____
_____

Finding God

Dear Madison,

This, in many ways, is the letter that took the most time and was perhaps the most awkward to handle because my thoughts on God and religion differ so dramatically from so many others.

I have been a seeker my entire life, although I didn't realize it at the time. There is an old saying that God doesn't leave you, you leave God, and this has been true for me during the course of my life. In my younger days at home with my mother, we visited many churches and were part of many religions, which I came to realize through the years are just different ways to find and approach God.

My mother tried many churches, but she was eventually disappointed in each one, and we were part of this progressive pilgrimage for her search for the perfect church, with the perfect group of worshippers, something that never existed, but that she nevertheless kept looking for in her life. The value in this to me was that I was exposed to many different ways to find God and often sat with my mouth open in church, marveling at the many different ways people decide to worship.

While this quest proved to be important in my never-ending search for questions that hadn't even revealed themselves to me yet, there was never a final moment when I knew that this person, or this approach, was the answer for me. Everyone at every church preached that his or her way was the only way, but how could a God capable of creating this world of billions of people hand out so few keys to his door? Preaching absolutes always drove me away from any church, but I never lost the need to find the answers for myself, nor did I ever lose sight that I believed in a higher power, although I was often in my youth a terrible example of the true nature of a caring and giving God.

Perhaps the enlightenment that will come to you someday will be the same that eventually appeared to me: There is no one way to seek God, and most of what man says about God was said to benefit man and the selfish course the writer or speaker wanted you to take. This has little to do about recognizing that a higher power exists, and should be part of your life, and is more about man's ego and need to control others through inciting a fear of a God that only this person knows, and if you simply follow this alleged conduit to the hidden gods of the universe, and send a big donation too, all will be revealed to you.

The personal enlightenment for me was when I used most of what was written by man as merely guides to help me along the journey and rise above the often pettiness in those books that create a life lived in someone else's mold. There hasn't ever been a day in my life without a conversation with God, but I had to seek Him on my own, and learn about what the universe has to offer someone willing to spend the time needed to dedicate his or her life to the quest.

During the course of this search, I read the Bible, the Koran, a large number of Buddhist books, many writings on the teachings and interpretations of Jesus, and a varied litany of works on most of the major religions in the world. This search gave me confidence that the quest was valid and that to find God, you have to rise above man and seek Him personally.

My life has been blessed, and when I have failed, there was always another solution or way to move forward that presented itself when most needed—to me, the touch of a forgiving God who once again forgave me for stupidity and bailed me out of yet another seemingly hopeless predicament. My business success has been based on a weird, eclectic variety of talents that have kept me fed and financially able to live life on my own terms for most of my adult life. Whatever creativity, talent, or skills I possess, I always felt I owed for them, and this always led me back to focusing on what I had to do every day, which was to help people change their lives when what they were doing just wasn't working for them.

All this, and more, including you and our family, has come to me as part of this search. There is a higher power, Madison, but the journey to find Him will, and should, take the rest of your life. Don't be afraid to believe, but also don't be afraid to question everything. Your life has to be your own journey, and make sure that part of that exploration is seeking a higher truth not ruined by any single man or religion.

1. What do you believe and why?

2. What would you like to teach others about your beliefs?

3. What have you learned about religion and faith in your life?

4. Write a letter to your children in the future about how you hope they practice faith and what you think they should someday believe.

Your life, your family

Your life, your family

Madison
at six

To my perfect granddaughter,

Being six years old is an awkward thing, and the year you were six was no exception to that rule. Your sixth summer was a year of wearing dresses every day and followed by a fall season adjusting to being a first grader—all while struggling with the last days of being mommy's baby. You lost your first tooth early in the fall, threw tantrums that would test the patience of a monk, realized you could read well for a child that age and proved it by making everyone sit and listen to you read about pigs, talking cows, and lost birds, and became one of the best spellers in your class. All told, you were a typical six-year-old kid we all loved dearly, but we still believed during that period that you were a tremendous pain in the ass.

Everyone talks about the terrible twos as the worst age for a parent to endure, but you made a case for the sassy sixes as the new leader in that race. This was also the year of learning to be friends with the other kids who had already grown into children who loved to be with other children and all the fun that entails.

Children all age differently. You can be six years old chronologically, meaning all six-year-old kids are six years old, but you can also biologically be four years old when you are six or even seven years old or older. Look at a picture of a classroom of six-year-olds, and some are taller, shorter, look older, act older, act younger, or might even be what is called the late bloomers, and while he or she is six, in many ways, he or she still looks and, most importantly, acts like a four-year-old. Kids are kids, but they all age mentally and physically at different rates.

Your sixth year was a transition year for you. When you were five, you bloomed and evolved from a quiet, shy child who struggled to interact with other kids to a young girl who made many friends and who loved to spend her time at parties and at the pool surrounded by your new group of other kids who all knew your name and who made you part of their groups.

When you were six, you faced the barrier many children have to struggle to get through in those early years. Mostly, you were always the youngest six-year-old in whatever group you were in—be it camp in the summer, dance class, or school. Being the youngest can be a good thing later in life, but when you are six, even a few months' maturity between kids can be a big thing.

But even by the end of summer, you had begun to change yet again, and with Nana's help, you started to find your place with the other kids. Nana sat with you many times that summer, explaining that the kids wouldn't want to be friends with someone who cried for their mother when they were dropped off or who clung to the young women who were the camp leaders that year. By the end of the summer, you were again one of the kids who leaped out of the car and ran off with the other kids with just a wave. Growing up is amazing, and watching you change so much over just a summer was startling, although you clung to those fleeting days of separation anxiety from your mother for most of that year.

Your sixth year was also a year of dance, beach days with the family, bicycle-riding with your new neighborhood friends, and afternoons at the pool with your grandmother. You spent about six weeks in camp that summer, singing, playing sports, and being in videos. You are probably still known as the only child whoever took a golf lesson that summer in a full dress with red shoes. You had your own style, and it was always in a dress and always with the special shoes to match.

Your Papa traveled a lot that year, and it was always shocking to come home and find how much you had changed. You were growing up before my eyes, which made me proud, but also sad that you were only going to be a little girl for such a short period of time. I often watched you do your workbooks that summer, and it was the first year that you read with ease and well above the level other kids that age usually read. Your Nana and mother were women of books, and neither one seldom missed a day that didn't include reading. You were also becoming that woman that summer, and you often went to the library and came home with three or four books that just had to be read with Nana over and over again.

There is a beauty in all children that many people never recognize. Your sixth summer was a summer of beauty for you. You were growing, healthy, curious, and, to a Papa that might be just a little prejudiced, the most beautiful child on the planet. Beauty is the combination of so many things, but often, we confuse physical beauty with true beauty.

You will be a physically beautiful woman when you grow up because the genes don't lie and your parents were good-looking, healthy people who gave birth to a perfect child. But your sixth summer was also a summer of discovering your hidden beauty. You became a friend to other kids, gained a confidence in yourself in dance, grew past being afraid of all the typical childhood fears, and discovered that you were good at a lot of things. It was your summer, Madison, and it flew by in minutes, lost to those memories of childhood.

Your sixth summer was the summer of Madison, and every child should have that one summer that makes his or her life special. You will have more magic summers, and I hope every summer is your summer for the rest of your life, but when you were six, you were magic, and I will miss that summer forever.

1. What do you remember about yourself when you were six?

2. Write a letter to your children in the future about how they are today. Add pictures, and do everything you can to capture them in time as they are just today.

3. Did you ever have a magic summer? What do you remember about it, and why was it special?

4. Write a short letter about who you are today and what you are doing in your life and then take a picture of yourself on every birthday, adding a new letter each year. This gives your children a way to see you as you were and who you are now.

5. Write a letter to your children about who they were when they were young, including all the small details that made them unique at that age.

Your life, your family

Money can't buy happiness

My dearest Madison,

One of the harshest lessons to understand in life is that most personal pain is self-inflicted. This is not referring to physical pain, but rather to the deep personal unhappiness that traps and eventually smothers the best in people.

You will find in your life that happiness eludes far more people than you would ever think, and as you grow through the years, you will find fewer and fewer people who ever claim to be truly happy. In fact, most of those you will encounter through work and friendships will live in a constant state of miserableness and wear their unhappy days like it's something to bear with pride. Asking "How are you doing today?" is met with a litany of complaints about bosses, spouses, children, the current person in politics who is stopping this person from getting his or her fair share, and, of course, the endless medical pain that comes from daily life. You asked, and you heard, and now you might be sorry you asked.

Most of this internal unhappiness becomes obvious to the person when he or she is in their 30s and 40s, which is a time when people stall in their careers, in their personal development, and often in their relationships with others. The seeds of this discontent can be sown when the person is younger, but it is during these years, when you should be enjoying life at the highest level, that many people then find happiness has eluded them, and there is nothing left in their souls but a deep pain that seems to have no answer or solution.

The realization of this unhappiness is often triggered when you first contemplate that what you are doing with your life today fails to match the hopes and dreams you had for yourself compared to who you actually became in life. The fear stems from the intellectual understanding that you are unhappy, and that you still have those dreams, but you are trapped in your current life, and the path you are on will never take you to the gate where those dreams are hidden.

My advice to you, my dearest child, is to avoid this trap by seeking a lifestyle of the minimalist. Going minimalist doesn't mean you give all your worldly possessions away, live naked in the woods, and end up begging for food from terrified tourists. What going minimalist really should mean is that you question carefully why you are carrying all the baggage in your life that causes this unhappiness and then get moving, trying to eliminate everyone and everything that has a negative effect on who you are and, most importantly, who you want to be in the future.

I called this baggage "rocks in a backpack," which to me is anything anchoring you down in life and preventing you from truly living your life on your own terms. Dropping this baggage also keeps you from seeking a fulfillment not found from endlessly trying to buy happiness through possessions—large and small—that drain your money and keep you endlessly chasing the next bright and shiny thing.

Another way to think about this analogy is that someone simply woke up one day and found him or herself trapped by his or her inability to control his or her career, money, and personal life and, therefore, control his or her life, and all these issues piled on your soul feels like you are carrying around a huge pack full of heavy rocks that no one is interested in helping you carry or unload.

The trap buried in this life is this person started on a cycle that continually feeds the unhappiness, and this cycle is always based on the need to constantly chase the next level of being happy by attempting to buy it. This cycle starts in his or her head with self-talk, such as "If I made more money, I would be happier than I am now," so the person works harder doing work he or she may not really like to make more money.

This newly generated money is spent on new cars, each one more expensive than the last, bigger houses, bigger televisions, more clothes and possessions, and all the trappings of happiness that are promoted through ads and through the culture. If you just buy this one great product, the ads claim, then you will at last find happiness in your life—at least until next year, when we run ads telling you that what you bought from us now is horribly out of date, and you can't live without replacing it for the current, must-have-it-now model.

New, bright, shiny, bigger, better, "got to have it," and "If I buy it, I will be happy" always fail over time because you simply can't buy enough to reach the end of the cycle, but this endless loop is the one that everyone who first makes money falls into at some point in his or her life. This is the pack full of rocks that kills careers, kills dreams, destroys relationships, and ultimately ends the ability to enjoy a fulfilled life.

It seems old school, and perhaps it is, as I find myself already an older man writing to his granddaughter years into the future, and by the time you read this, you will have certainly heard this advice before, but you can't buy happiness, and the acquisition of all the stuff in the world has never resulted in long-term happiness for anyone.

The day you discover happiness is "less stuff and more you" will be the day you find personal freedom. Stop spending what you haven't yet earned, and start understanding that living with less in your life is often the most you can possibly ever own.

Living minimalist is easy, but the first step is often difficult, especially if you have already started down the wrong path. First of all, take a few days to list the rocks in your life. Is your mortgage too big, and you bought the big house because you felt it would make you happy, and now you are working harder and longer to pay for a house where you are never home? Did that new car, with the big payment, fail to make you as silly happy as the ads promised? Is that toxic person in your life preventing you from reaching your dreams?

While you are identifying the rocks, take time to also write out a list of what truly makes you happy. If this list is honest, and from the heart, you will find such things on the list as "time with family" or "more time to work out" rather than "Buy more stuff on a credit card with money I have to make next week."

I hope you find as I have that happiness is usually defined as personal action and experience and seldom as the acquisition of more stuff. For example, more days spent skiing or at the beach, quiet time spent reading, and even time with a herd of screaming kids at a theme park are all more valuable than another electronic gadget or this year's must-have purse or car.

One of the biggest things that will hurt you and your family is debt. Debt is almost always acquired by spending money, usually on credit cards, that you haven't yet made through work. But debt can also be buying more than you need or living beyond your ability to ever make enough money to pay it all off. Question every purchase, and question that part of human nature that finds you at the mall spending money to just make yourself feel better for a while.

People spend because the act of spending seems so satisfying, but that thrill lasts mere minutes, and there is nothing for that person but to do it again, hoping for the same short-term thrill that will again quickly fade. You might do this because you are mad at someone, sad, depressed over something at work, or merely want to pamper yourself for a few hours. What you spend now is something you will have to work for and then pay for over time, and you will find all those small purchases can add up to large amounts of debt.

As I have said in many of the other letters in this book, money is freedom. Saving money, and having money put away, allows you to leave a job you don't like, take a risk and start your own business, or take a few months off and travel the coast of Australia or go on some other adventure that tickles your passion. Money exists for only one reason: You can get up every day and do whatever you like on your own terms without anyone holding you to a job or situation you don't like because you are trapped by the load of paying off bills for all the stuff you own. In this case, you might realize you don't really own stuff—the stuff owns you.

Another important part of living a minimalist life is the elimination of clutter in your life. When I was young, I discovered books, and the lifetime pleasure of reading and having bookcases and piles of books wherever I lived became one of the more comforting things in my life.

And then I realized later that the books sat on shelves, often unread ever again, and these trusted friends were becoming a burden to be cared for and carried from home to home. I also realized there were people who could benefit from those books and who would enjoy them much more than I did by merely looking at them on shelves, so I ended up donating most to the library and gave the others away, except for a small shelf of favorites that I would reread every few years.

This advice also goes for those old clothes strangling your closet that would be warmly received at the local shelter as well as all that stuff in the basement in those boxes that have remained unopened since your college dorm days. Old memories are always the mental block for many people, such as boxes of old pictures or mementoes from another period in your life. Scan the pictures; photograph the stuff that means something, but if you haven't had it out of the box in years, move it on too. Less is more, and most everything someone would collect can be replaced. You will have stuff in your life, but less stuff gives you a huge advantage to travel, to be flexible where you live, and to pack up and take that next adventure.

Toxic people in your life also need to go. Going minimalist is not something restricted to just tangible objects. Going minimalist, and getting the rocks out of the backpack, also means that all those toxic relationships in your life need to be cleared out. It was always surprising to listen to someone talking who spends the better part of an hour explaining (or justifying) why he or she can't change the challenging issues in his or her life because of his or her relationship with someone who is totally toxic and fights every move he or she makes to seek a better path and a better life.

Toxic people are usually people who are miserable in their own lives, and by the power of everything bad in the universe, they want to make you miserable too. Toxic people are the ones who tell you that new idea or dream won't work, you will fail if you take risks, you are not bright enough to reach that dream, you aren't trustworthy enough to go out with your friends, and you are better staying in your place rather than trying to be something you are not.

Toxic people hate your dream of success because when you get to a higher level, they now have to face the reality of their own miserable, nonproductive existence. Start eliminating all toxicity by eliminating the people who are exerting the most pressure to drag you under the bus. You will have many beautiful friends in your life, but you will also realize some people who appear to be your friend will do a lot to make sure you go nowhere and achieve nothing because if you reach and grow, their unwillingness to change or try becomes so much more apparent.

The hardest part of this, of course, is you may be related to many of these people and might even be married to one. Relatives who are trapped in their own lives seldom realize there is a way out, and the same rule also applies to them; distance yourself as best you can, and listen to nothing negative that escapes from their mouths. Your dreams must always remain your dreams, and sometimes, the best path to reach what you want is to ignore those who try to discourage you the most.

When it comes to a spouse, you must answer the hardest of all questions: Can I reach the goals in my life in five years with this person at my side? If the answer is no, pack what little stuff you have left after reading this letter (another great time to edit down the unneeded possessions), and hit the door running, and don't stop until you get to the point where you regain complete control of your life and your choices. Life is too short to fight the great battles without a true partner standing with you, and if your current choice is not the one, don't waste a lot of time trying to change the person—just understand that you might have chosen badly and that it is time to move on.

I believe you must also eliminate anything stopping the power of your mind. You can live without a television, and you can survive without being wired to the universe 24/7. Try turning off your television for one month, and try leaving your cell phone off for three-hour blocks throughout the day. In fact, walk in the door, look at your kid or dog, and then decide if one hour in the park with either one could be vastly improved if you left the phone at home.

As I write this, the average television is on seven-and-a-half hours a day, which means the average mind watching a television is off for seven-and-a-half hours per day. Read, sit quietly, think or meditate, work out more, or sit in front of a fire with the one you love, and drink a glass of wine, and talk about how great life can be. In other words, do anything that keeps you engaged in life, and eliminate any rock that keeps your mind numb or tied to something that doesn't enhance who you are and what you want.

Your job might become the biggest rock on your back. It is a vicious circle in a normal overstuffed life. You need money to pay for the stuff you don't need, so you work at a job you don't like to pay the bills for stuff you bought with the money you hadn't made yet, and you can't leave the job you don't like because you can't save enough money to try something new because you can't escape from under the huge pile of rocks you are lugging.

Stuff traps you in jobs you hate, and nothing will drain the creativity and passion out of a human being faster than spending a couple years' time working in a job you can't stand, or for people you don't respect. It may take you time to move on, but if you ever find yourself doing work that isn't your passion, then spend every waking hour paying off debt or learning the skills it takes to get out while your mind is still alive.

You also need to learn that less stuff, and fewer bills, allows you to make less in a job you really love instead of always trying to seek the next best-paying job that only enables you to pay for the bright and shiny stuff that will never fulfill you anyway. You are defined by your life's work, my love, and your contribution to the world will come from the passion you bring to how you choose to make a living.

In case no one has ever told you, or ever given you permission before, you can have it all. You can have a career that makes you excited to get up in the morning, and you can make enough money to live life on your own terms, but you first have to drop the rocks keeping you trapped doing something that merely eats the days of your life.

Finally, live for the experiences in life. You can spend money, and you don't have to live the life of a monk holed up in the woods preaching to squirrels by going minimalist, but how you spend this money is what is important. The next time you are considering replacing a car that is only a few years old because you are bored with it, or you are standing at the local electronics retailer thinking about getting a bigger television to replace the perfectly good, but smaller, one at home, head to the local coffee shop and write down five adventures or experiences you could have for the same money.

The money spent on a television represents a brilliant play and dinner for two or that money is a mountain bike camp in the Rockies. That money could also be a full day with the kids doing something crazy, such as rafting the local river or exploring the zoo. That money is also a quiet weekend in a good hotel for you and the significant person in your life, and if you are really lucky, you spend that weekend in the room drinking great champagne and never leaving the room, dreaming dreams and quietly cherishing each other's time.

You will read this when you are young, but know now that no one ever lay dying in a hospital and her last regret was "I wish I would have bought one more big television." What that person would regret is a life without adventures and a life without experiences. Use your time, which is the most precious of all the things you own, to see the world and to have the adventures that last for a lifetime.

Remember just one thing from all this: Living with less is often the most you can ever have in your life. Live well, my child, and live a life fulfilled.

1. Much of personal pain is often self-inflicted. What mistakes have you made that have had a negative effect on your life?

2. Have you ever felt trapped in a job or a career?

3. Have you ever felt trapped by spending too much on things you really don't need or want but now have to pay for later?

4. What is in your backpack these days that is holding your life back?

5. What does "less stuff, more you" mean to you in your life?

6. How do you feel about debt in your life, and what experiences have you had that might help others in the future?

7. What does "going minimalist" mean to you?

8. Write a letter to your children in the future as to how you hope they live in a world where "The more you have, the more you want" is a way of life.

Your life, your family

Your life, your family

A time to be still

Dear Madison,

Learning to be still, finding quiet time, and allowing yourself to heal from the pressures of the real world may be difficult things to learn, especially in the world as it exists today with the need to be connected every hour and every minute of every day.

Along with the ability to stay connected comes the inability to be able to find time that is just yours. The mind, and the body, needs quiet time to heal and reenergize, and that is virtually impossible when you are constantly wired to the universe.

When you were child of five, you had already found that you were good at most things computer and were able even then to operate iPads®, find things on the Internet, and manipulate your way through dozens of computer games. In fact, just prior to your sixth birthday, you surprised your mother by going online and finding videos of a musician you had heard her reference while she was in another room. You had just started reading and were able to spell out enough of the person's name to find a video. You were better at a computer when you were five than Nana was when she was 50.

In today's society, and it will only get more intense in the future when you are most likely reading this, people have lost the sense of personal time and personal space and also the ability to live within the moment. Perhaps the best example of losing the moment might be two people who go to dinner together and then spend the entire time on personal devices that keep them connected with people who are elsewhere. Did you watch and become engaged in the concert, or did you simply video it on your phone and miss the music and energy? Did you takes endless photos of your kid at the beach, or did you walk in the surf, feel the water, and lay happily in the sun, fully engaged in what you were doing?

Living in the moment is a simple concept: Where you are is where you should focus. If you care for someone enough to spend an hour with him or her, then living in the moment means this person is the focus of that hour. If you are skiing, be aware of the mountain, the wind, and the crunch of the snow, the sounds of lifts and other skiers, and everything else that makes that experience unique.

Being there, but trying to be somewhere else by letting your thoughts drift away to a business problem, school issue, a worry about your child or friend, or anything else that takes you out of the moment, is a horrible waste of the experience, and as you get older, you will realize that the real value in life is a life filled with experiences, not things, and experiences will be what shapes and defines you as a person.

The time to be still can be as simple as 15 minutes of quiet meditation each day or a run in the woods, or as complex as a week spent driving across the country by yourself to see a friend. Time spent being quiet, or off the grid as we currently say, means that for just a short time, the phones are turned off, the computers are down, and the world is yours and yours alone for as much time as you can steal.

It is vitally important to find time to think. So many people are so busy being busy that taking time to sit and quietly think about their lives is a lost art. Lost days turn into lost weeks and then lost years. You can be so busy that you never really get anything done that is important. One of the most important things you could do would be to get up a little earlier and spend an hour with a cup of tea or coffee and a journal and a pen, locked in a room with no electronic stimulation, and just write about what you want, how you feel, and where you want to be in life.

Do it before your friends start calling you to be part of their day. Do this before the kids get up and your day is filled with all things in their lives. Do it before you have to go change someone else's life in your job, and do it before the world finds out you are up and thinking. Quiet time is one of the single most important things you need to stay whole and fresh, but is always one of those things that is the farthest down our list to do. Find that time today and every day; you are worth it.

Value yourself, and those who are important in your life, by finding time to sit quietly and live within those moments focused on nothing more but being you.

1. Do you allow yourself to have quiet time?

2. Do you ever "go off the grid" and just spend time alone without electronic gadgets constantly trying to interrupt your peace?

3. What is your biggest time-waster, and does it affect your life?

4. When do you find time to think?

5. What would you teach others about finding quiet time in their lives?

Your life, your family

Your life, your family

Do what you say you will do

My forever little Madison,

Promise little to anyone, but do everything you promise. These have always been powerful words to me, and have guided my life for much of my later years, but very few people you will meet in your life will honor these simple words. In fact, most live their lives doing the complete opposite: promising to do everything for anyone who asks, committing to being everywhere and doing everything, but in reality never living up to their words. Often, you will find that people promise anything in hopes they will be liked or loved and then fail to live up to those hollow promises given too often and too lightly.

The application of this short sentence is quite wide. Promising little, but doing everything you promise, applies to commitments to friends and also to a much higher level of trust. Friends will come and go through your life, but each friend you have should be treated with value until that person is no longer your friend. Giving your word, by promising you will do something, should never be done lightly.

If you promise to help a friend move to another home, and you commit to be there, then someone is counting on you, and you should honor that commitment. If a friend asks for a ride, and you promise your time, then that promise becomes something you have committed to with someone who is important in your life, and you must do what you said you will do. If you can't keep a commitment, but promised the person just to make someone happy for a short period of time, then you should never give that commitment in the first place because you will inevitably break the trust. Promise only what you are willing to do, and never anything more, with friends and others in your life.

This small thought also applies to life at a higher level. Someday, you might get married, and this rule applies. If you promise to be there for someone by committing to be with that person as partners for life, then never enter into that relationship without thinking about what you are truly promising someone. Only promise what you know you can do. Many people fail at this when they are young, including me, because they do not project themselves into a life far into the future. Yes, someday, you might give a promise you will be unable to keep, but this does not mean any promise should be given without thought and awareness.

Someday, you will also start a career, and this rule represents the bond of trust between someone who hires you and what you bring to that job. Any job is important, and there are no small jobs. If you are hired to do something, you are making this commitment to the person who hired you. If the employer turns out to be horrible, and if the job is not what you want, then leave, but while you are there, keep your commitment by being the best you can be. Just because an employer fails does not mean you now have permission to be a lesser version of yourself. Live with respect for yourself, and for those who give you an opportunity, and remember that you are always better to leave that situation rather than lower your standards.

My dear Madison, become the person people trust and count on in their lives, and become the person who lives by a higher personal standard based on your willingness to do what you promise. Never promise what you can't, or won't, do, and always do what you promise.

114

1. Promise little to anyone, but do everything you promise. What does this mean to you? Do you live your life this way or are you one of those people who promises too much and then has a hard time keeping those promises?

2. Do you believe that your commitments to others are important to keep?

3. What would you teach others about broken promises and commitments?

4. Have you ever had someone break his or her word to you, and how did that feel? What did you learn from that experience?

5. Keeping your commitments is considered a sign of a mature adult. Write a letter to your children in the future that talks about how you feel about making commitments in your life.

Your life, your family

Your life, your family

Nana

My most beautiful granddaughter,

This letter is a struggle for me to write because it is about your grandmother, a woman who could inspire a book, but I somehow have to capture a sense of her for you in just a few pages.

Your Nana was a third-generation Cape Cod woman, reared from strong, independent women who lived lives decades ahead of what was accepted in the culture of their times. Your great-great-grandmother and your great-grandmother were women who lived within what was considered the right thing to do at the time, but also lived and excelled living outside the lines. Your great-grandmother, for example, was a strong wife and supporter of her husband as he built homes and created businesses on the cape, but she was also an independent woman who traveled the world on her own, leaving him home while she ventured off to China and Europe.

This streak of independence is important to note because your Nana was yet another woman of the same mold who also lived a dual life as a wife and life partner while still being true to her heritage.

Your grandmother opened a business in a male-dominated field almost 30 years before it became truly accepted for women to compete equally in the field of fitness. Her business was not just owning a fitness facility for women, which is secondary to the story, but rather her true business was creating a place where women could meet safely, get help and nurturing as they sought to improve their lives through better health, and get true information centered on women and their special needs as they pursued a healthy life.

Your Nana was a considerable force in business, something she definitely inherited from her father. The joke was often that your grandmother was the best businessman in the family, something your great-grandfather slowly came to admit and then admire as he aged himself. He grew up in an era where women stayed home to raise a family and the man provided. It took years, and he was a man of 80 before he could smile and admire your Nana as a woman who had made her own way in business.

He was also trapped in the way things were in the era he grew up. In his day, as a young man, the woman raised kids, stayed home, ironed shirts, and played a secondary role to her own wants and needs. His wife, who was your great-grandmother Polly, lived this role, but she was also independent. Your great-grandfather Jim accepted this slowly, but it was a struggle for him because her independence went against everything he was ever taught. After your great-grandmother passed away, he finally came to accept, and then enjoy, the fact that his daughter, your Nana, was her own woman and as good at business as he was. Times change, but slowly, and she stayed true to her roots by succeeding on her own in her own business.

Nana could have done many other things in her life if she had chosen and perhaps if the culture of that time period had been different. She had a very linear mind that would have suited being a doctor or an attorney, but she could have also followed your grandfather, who had a law degree but never chose to practice, and built homes on the cape. Her talent was deep, and she found an outlet for this talent in business.

Nana was also a woman of books. There was never a time in all the years we were together that she was without at least several different books going at the same time. She was a voracious reader, something your mother inherited, and could finish a book in a day or two if it interested her. Her quiet time, something you will need to master in your life, was always about soft pajamas, a good book, music, and a glass of wine. These hours were her way of finding peace in her life, and these lost hours also became some of the fondest memories of my life with her.

The years with Nana were the best years in my life. My businesses struggled in our early years, my journey was at times chaotic living a life on the road, and we were both damaged people when we met in ways that would be hard to describe. As you age, granddaughter, you will begin to realize life is never a straight line of happiness, but rather a long rolling line with peaks of greatness followed by struggles and the low points. If you find the right partner in your life, facing the down slopes can many times be easier and the tough times not so tough if you wander through life holding the hand of someone you love deeply. This worked for me with Nana, and I believe that much of what I accomplished in life would have never have happened if it would have been a life without her.

In many ways, we were people who were almost too much alike. Uniting two strong-willed people who have built their own businesses seems like a prescription for disaster, but over time, we found ways to support each other, and I believe our strength together as two was greater than the individual parts. Look around you, and you will see this in others. For every failure in a partnership of life, you will find people who get together, and their combined strength allows them to rise to another level other couples can't achieve. Be slow and be patient in love, and you will someday find the person that allows you to always be you, but together, you can accomplish great things.

When you think of your Nana, always remember three things about her. First of all, despite her small size, she was an extremely talented businesswoman who defied all the rules of the time and understood how to make money and take care of herself and her family. Someday, my child, you will consider your own career, and when you do, remember that the women in your family were born to be independent and create things done their way.

Secondly, remember that she was a woman who overcame a lot of sadness in her early life. Every woman at some time or another is faced with times in her life where it seems nothing she does will matter and that there is no way to escape the darkness that sometimes falls over good people. Your grandmother was a tough woman who managed to come through an abusive relationship that sadly other women might have remained trapped in for the rest of their life. Tough times will always end, and tough women always come through to the light. When you face struggles in your life, remember that there is no light without darkness and that you will find the strength to keep going to better times.

Thirdly, remember that your Nana was a woman who willing to stand up for herself. She accepted responsibility for her own life when things were not going well and never blamed anyone for the things under her own control. She made mistakes, but kept going through difficult times. She was also generous and gracious, and she always lived within herself.

Accepting full responsibility for who you are and what you do, good and bad, has always been limited to a small number of people, but there is no other way to live your life on this Earth that is more powerful. Your Nana understood this, lived this way, and, most important, always held others to that high standard—something that was often new to other people who live life by blaming others for their failings.

You are the granddaughter of a strong and beautiful woman, and your heritage will be one of strength and beauty in your own life. Remember the lessons from Nana's life. Take responsibility for all you are, love graciously, enjoy a good book with a glass of wine, and never forget that you come from a line of women who have always sought to change the world around them. This is who you are, Madison, and this is the gift Nana has given you.

122

1. How do you remember your parents? What would you like others to know about them? What lessons could others learn from their lives?

2. What are the important things you want your children to remember about your parents? Have you taken pictures and created a life story for each one to pass along to others someday?

3. What other aspects of your heritage are important not to lose, and what do you want to pass along someday to others?

4. Write a detailed letter about each parent, including pictures, and seal it away to pass along someday to your children.

5. Document your own life now as if you were going to pass along who you are to your grandchildren someday. What do you want them to remember of you, how you lived, and what you believed?

Your life, your family

Your life, your family

_____
_____
_____
_____
_____
_____
_____
_____
_____
_____
_____
_____
_____
_____
_____
_____
_____
_____
_____
_____
_____
_____

Life in motion

Dear Madison,

One of the things I want to teach you, my granddaughter, is to always live a life in motion. The concept of a life in motion is that you are always projecting your life ahead of today, dreaming dreams to realize and goals to achieve, and then you always live a life that moves those hopes and dreams forward.

Most people have no idea what they want from the experience of their life. These people live a random life, usually taking what rolls their way and living day by day, but seldom ever living a satisfying or fulfilling life. Their dreams and desires remain hidden, and eventually lost, because they never took the time, or had the courage, to sit quietly and think about what they want from their lives. Madison, you can survive by simply trying to be happy with what is given to you, or you can spend life chasing what you want and what is important to you. Both ways are choices you make, but only one can make you truly happy over time.

This is one of my favorite quotes I used often when I was trying to get people to start thinking about what they were trying to accomplish in their lives. People would call me looking for help and guidance, but before we could discuss any type of help, we had to always ascertain just what we were going to try to get done.

This quote was a strong way to get that discussion going. My first statement to anyone looking for help was "I can help you get anywhere you want to go, and we will find a way to get it done, but if you don't know where you are going, then no one can help you get there." This quote is from *Alice's Adventures in Wonderland* by Lewis Carroll, and it always helped me get people focused on finding their dreams:

> Alice came to a fork in the road. "Which road do I take?" she asked.
>
> "Where do you want to go?" responded the Cheshire Cat.
>
> "I don't know," Alice answered.
>
> "Then," said the Cat, "it doesn't matter."

This perfectly illustrates how many people proceed through their lives: no chosen road, no path, no direction, and no hope of ever accomplishing anything important because they never know what they want to accomplish. Their dreams remain just fantasies—something used as an escape to a temporary better life five minutes before you fall asleep and destined to remain just an illusion that never becomes real.

As in most everything, I had a system for getting this done in my own life. Every three months, I would escape to the local coffee shop and sit and write for several hours, constantly trying to project my life, and what I wanted from it, ahead into the future. Even though I lived and worked through the latest computers all of my life, this labor of love was always done with old-fashioned notebooks and pens. There is something more personal when pen touches paper, especially when you are writing about what you want from being you.

My writings were based on a simple concept: I would project my life ahead one year, three years, five years, and 10 years, and the categories always remained the same. What did I want financially from my life, what did I want through personal development, what did I want from my career, and what did I want from the experiences of my life?

Figuring out what I wanted from each of these categories, and then projecting what I wanted through so many years, forced me to set specific goals that were important to me while helping me eliminate other ideas that faded once compared to others on the list. Doing this every three months, for more than 30 years, gave me a sense of direction and kept me on track. For more than 20 years, until the invention of iPads, there was never a day I didn't walk out of the house with three small cards in my pocket. Each card had something I had to get done that day to move my life ahead somehow. Just accomplishing three things a day that are important leads to a life rich and fulfilled.

The common belief you will often hear is that people are who they are due to the decisions they make in their lives. I believe this is a false statement, and stating it this way does more harm than good for someone. You are who you are, Madison, not because of the decisions you made, but because of the hard decisions you failed to make.

If you don't know what you want, then every decision you make in your life will always be based on the path of least resistance. Why make a decision that is difficult if you have no sense of where it leads and how it affects what you are trying to get done through the years? We fail because we never make the big decisions that have to be made and then commit to the hard work that comes with tough choices. You can't make sound decisions and choices in your life, and support those around you, if you don't know whether the opportunity in front of you today helps or works against your goals and what you wanted to get accomplished.

Goal setting, my child, is about becoming an artist. Your life is a chance to create a beautiful painting as you envision it. The canvas is blank and represents your life, and you can create any masterpiece, done in your own style and by your own hand, you want.

Never let anyone else paint on your canvas. Never let anyone else dictate your style. If you need help figuring out who you are or where you are going, seek a mentor, and perhaps the pages of this book, which might help you achieve your personal style of painting, but ultimately, when your life is through, the painting will be your gift to others, and its pattern and colors must remain true to you.

1. What does living a life in motion mean to you?

2. What do you want from the experience of being you? What major goals do you have in life? Where do you see yourself in five years, 10 years, and beyond?

3. What would you like to be remembered for at the end of your life? How would you like your children to explain who you were and what you accomplished in life?

4. What does living a life that matters mean to you? How would you explain that to others?

5. Sit quietly while you write the things you most want to accomplish in your life. What do you want from your work? Want do you want from family? What you want financially? What do you want spiritually?

6. You can have anything you want, but you can't have everything you want. What do you want if you only accomplish one big thing in your life?

Your life, your family

*Value
your life*

My dearest Madison,

No one lives forever, although most people tend to live and make choices as if they believe they will. At some point in your life, most of the people who you love the most in life will be gone. As we age, we often lose the ones who have given us life, and each succeeding generation ultimately ends up replacing those who have gone before them with the next line of people who always believe they will be the first generation that will live forever.

The fact that everyone eventually dies is a fact of the universe, and there is nothing you can do to change that law, but you do have the most important choice, and only you can make this decision, as to how well you chose to live within whatever years you have coming.

Valuing your life means you realize that every day is unique, precious, and irreplaceable, and it is your obligation to yourself to value who you are and your uniqueness on this planet. There is only one you, you have only one finite life, and only you can make the decision to value yourself enough that you never waste a single second of something so precious.

Valuing your life is also about making decisions starting early that allow you to achieve the most, and live the fullest life possible, in your years. Valuing your life means you learn to eat well so your years are spent in health and not wasted in self-induced sickness. Valuing your life means you live a life in motion, constantly seeking an advanced level of fitness that will extend your active and productive years well past those who have avoided the personal responsibility it takes to live at such a high personal standard.

Valuing life is not avoiding risks and living a quiet, safe life hidden in a closet so you might never get hurt, but rather chasing life and managing the risks that are associated with living life at the highest threshold. These choices might be as mundane as wearing a helmet on a ski slope, avoiding drugs that can alter and shorten your life and degrade who you are, or avoiding a certain street at night. There is risk in almost everything, but there is no life worth living without risk and understanding, and managing risk is far more essential than trying to avoid it altogether.

To me, there have always been only three ways to achieve a life based on personal value. First of all, seek the healthiest lifestyle you can achieve that will in fact negate much of the aging process through the years. In other words, you will always only be as young as your body and mind feels, and lifetime fitness and personal growth will keep both of those parts of your life fresh while others falter.

Secondly, and this will be written about in another letter to you, learn to live life on your own terms. Being who you are, and who you were meant to be, is perhaps life's greatest personal achievement in a world where it seems everyone and everything is trying to force you to be someone else.

Thirdly, seek the adventure. Your life is meant to be lived on the stage of life, not something to be viewed from a lousy seat in the audience. Nothing can replace the power of a personal experience doing something new and wonderful, and the experiences of your life will at some point become far more valuable to you than any bright, shiny object or purchase. Experience is life, so use your time and your money to chase the adventures that will define who you are and who you will be.

Live large, child. Nothing was ever achieved by living in moderation. The adventures of life are out there on the edges. The birth of your child, the day you were married, and the day you achieved the biggest goals and dreams are all highlights and the best days you will have. But there are also the small things that are remembered as big in your life. Sunsets at the beach, a run at dawn in a strange new city, or just a quiet walk with someone you love are all small, but all so big.

You can't describe sitting on a mountaintop in Colorado after a six-hour hike with friends as a moderate day, nor could you describe the birth of your granddaughter as one either. These are the big moments, and I hope you live for the taste of these in life and do everything you can to make sure your life is filled with the big days and big adventures, along with those small remembrances that will remain with you always.

1. What choices can a person make that shows he or she values his or her life? What bad choices do people make that show lack of respect for their own lives?

2. What does healthy living mean to you?

3. The choices you make each day determine the quality of your life in the future. Are there better choices you could make now? What does this statement mean to you and your personal future?

4. What kind of choices would you want your children to make in their futures? Most children learn their lifestyles from their parents. What will they learn from you and how you live?

5. What are the five biggest habits you need to change to show value for your own life? Fitness? Food? Personal growth and development? Toxic people and relationships?

6. You are tomorrow what you choose to do today. What kind of choices do you make each day, and who will you be tomorrow?

Your life, your family

Your life, your family

Living within yourself

Dear Madison,

One of the most difficult things you will find in life to achieve is the ability to live within yourself. Living within yourself simply means you live your own life, chasing your own dreams, and most of your motivation and direction for this trek comes from your own sense of who you are and what you want.

Many people spend their lives surrounded by friends, family, and perhaps that person who becomes the significant love in your life. I hope you are blessed this way and that you are always part of a group of people who love you and who care about who you are and what you want.

There is a negative, however, to this group of people who seemingly always want what is best for you, and that negative is that what others want for you is often based on their own personal agendas, inadequacies, and failures in their own lives. Often, these people attempt to guide you down a path that is "best for you," and it always appears they are trying to get you to do "the right thing," but often, the right thing is really what is best for them and often not something good for you. There are real mentors out there who do care about what is best for you, and this group spends its time helping you stay on the path you chose, or might even help you find the path itself if needed.

As you grow and start on your own path, you will often receive advice filled full of words and phrases, such as "should," "Aren't you concerned about what others think?" or "You have to do the right thing here." These are words others use to create guilt in your mind and seldom have little to do with who you are and what you are trying to accomplish. Doing the right thing often means doing what that person wants you to do and seldom really has any relationship to what is truly right and wrong in life as it pertains to your goals, ethics, and personal code of conduct.

As you mature in life, understand that as you achieve success, others in your life—and realize that some of these people will often be very close to you—will not want you to succeed. If you are surrounded by a close group of friends from school, for example, as you grow, there will always be those in the group who fail or don't even try in life.

These anchors around your waist will often resent your success because what you are doing in life highlights their failures. In other words, the more you succeed, the brighter the light shines on those around you who aren't growing or moving farther down the path. These people resent your success and often work quite hard to make sure you don't achieve your dreams. The light shines poorly on this group, and most will do most anything to deflect the pressure of personal growth to someone else.

No, these people are not bad people, and most of them seldom realize that what they say to you is even negative, but there is often little difference between a group of supporting friends and an anchor that forever holds you down at the bottom of the sea. As you grow, there will be friends who will grow with you, and there will be friends who fall to the wayside, replaced by others who have made it to that higher level of growth and achievement as you have in your life.

As you become successful, you will attract others who are also enjoying their moment in the sun, and those people who can't take the pressure of being a friend of someone who is moving ahead in life will falter and quietly slip away from you. Sometimes, the best friends a person can have are those who are no longer in your life, and can no longer cause you pain through their envy and failure. In other words, their greatest gift to you as a friend might be to simply move on in their lives and stop holding you back from living yours.

Living within yourself merely states that significant others come and go and need to live their life, not yours. There will also be friends who enter your life and leave, or family who mostly care little about your success as compared to driving their own personal agendas that often have nothing to do with you and often reflect their own inadequacies and hidden plans for your life. You will experience all these people, and just knowing they are there will help you recognize and separate yourself from what you want and what they want for you.

Also, remember that many times, the advice you get from people older than you will be based on them attempting to accomplish their failed dreams by living through you. You will see children forced into sports or dance because the parent never accomplished his or her dreams in these activities. You will also see friends forced into careers that have little real interest to them, but their parents were accomplished in these areas; therefore, the children have to follow that path even if it has little value to what they want from their own lives. Always question advice, and ask yourself if what you are hearing is good for you, or just benefits the person giving the advice.

Living within yourself is just another way of saying that the only thing you will ever truly own in your life is what is between your ears. Talent and ability are rare, and resented by many, but these are the tools that define your life. Pushing to the end of your own abilities is what creates a life worth living, and no one should ever stand in the way of a man or woman chasing his or her own dreams.

Do what is best for you, and live life on your own terms, my perfect child. Avoid the words and phrases "should," "You have to," and the classic statement of guilt from generations past: "No one does that around here." There is nothing you have to do in your life except live it every day as you want to live it.

Follow your dreams, my sweet child, and no one else's. Do what you want, and never let anyone tell you what you should be doing with your life. You can learn from others' mistakes, and never be afraid of asking why others have struggled. Everyone has a lesson to teach, but most of these lessons won't always apply to you, and part of the growing process in your life will be the ability to carefully understand the difference between someone forcing his or her own agenda on you and someone else who merely wants you to learn from the mistakes he or she has made in his or her own life.

Perhaps the most important thing in life is to rise to your own talent and realize that those with less talent or ability will always conspire to keep you down at their level of comfort, which is often just a mediocre life, lived in quiet desperation. Getting older is often described as nothing more than a continual need to compromise for the rest of your life, and this is the biggest lie anyone could tell you. Few people live truly happy lives, but you will find those who do are living it on their own terms and have spent their lives, sometimes with success and sometimes with failure, on their own terms.

And most importantly, live within yourself. Eliminate from your life those who fight to keep you down, and make your life's decisions based on an internal motivation and self-awareness that no one can ever take from you.

1. What does living within yourself mean to you?

2. Are there people now in your life who resent your life and who you are? Are they holding you back from making decisions that would move your life ahead?

3. What would you do with your life if you lived it completely the way you want to live it? Why aren't you doing this?

4. What mistakes have you made letting others guide your life?

5. What would you want to teach your children about living life on their own terms? Write them a letter helping them understand how they should live when they are older.

Your life, your family

_____

_____

_____

_____

_____

_____

_____

_____

_____

_____

_____

_____

_____

_____

_____

_____

_____

_____

_____

_____

_____

_____

_____

Nothing lasts forever

Another letter to the perfect child,

This might be one of the most difficult letters to write, although I have started other letters in this book with these same words because many of the subjects here were hard for me to write and will be difficult for you to read. In this letter, I want to share with you one of the hardest lessons in life to understand, especially when you are young and the world seems to always be a place where the sun will rise, your life goes on, and tomorrow will happen. The reality of life— yours, mine, and everyone else in the world—is nothing lasts forever.

What this saying really explains is the concept of time and how it relates to your age in life. The younger you are, the more time you seem to have, and as you age, life accelerates and time eventually becomes the thing you have the least amount of in your possessions.

Another thought on this is when you are young, you always have the time to do anything, and any goal set will eventually be gotten to somewhere out there next year. The reality is, as you get older, you will find yourself out of time, and perhaps the first sign of recognizing your own mortality is that you have to begin to make choices for the first time in your life once you start to realize there simply isn't enough time left to accomplish everything on the list.

The fallacy in all this is believing that the young will live until they are old and that life progresses as in the storybooks. People pass away as a part of life, and you may live to be 100, or you may live to be 30. Only God knows, and He doesn't really share that information too readily, so you have to decide how to live your life fully each and every day. The key to a fulfilled life is to live every day as if it is your last. Plan for tomorrow, hope for tomorrow, be ready for tomorrow, but live within today.

This doesn't mean to spend all your money each day and not save. This doesn't mean you don't find meaningful work and prepare to be the best you can be. This does mean that when it comes to adventures, relationships, and risk, you should understand you have to deal with those things in the present, not somewhere in the future.

There was a young friend in my life named Scotty who died in his early 30s in a senseless accident. He was an accomplished rock climber, skier, and world-class friend to anyone who would spend just a few hours with him. His death left a big hole in many people's lives, and I can say now that his death taught me more about living than any other lesson I might have ever had. Scotty's death saddened everyone who had ever known him. He was young, energized, and caring, and he was cheated out of the chance to live of a long life, but those who knew him realized he had lived a full and meaningful life in his 30-some years. There was the thought of tomorrow for Scotty, but tomorrow wasn't as important as today, and he lived more in those short years than most people would accomplish if they lived to be 150.

Nothing lasts forever means that someday, none of us will be here. It also means that the bad times, and the good times, in your life are always just passing clouds and blow through your day to be eventually be replaced by the next one. When people have bad times, those horrible days feel like they will never end, but nothing lasts forever, and those too shall pass away. You also have to understand that when people are in the middle of the best days of their lives, those too will pass by, replaced by other clouds bringing something new and not always pleasant to your life. The bad and the good come and go, and life goes on. Endure the bad knowing that it will pass, and savor the good knowing that it will also end.

The lesson from Scotty was to live within the day. Stay in contact with those you love, and don't ever believe you can put that important call off to someone you love and miss until next week. Get up, get out, and get the most out of each day. If an adventure comes your way, don't wait until next year because next year just may not be there for you. Never go to bed mad at anyone, mend friendships today, reach out to those lost souls in your life now, and do not be afraid to risk what you have to get what you want.

Savor the good times in your life, Madison, and live each day on your terms, but understand that life changes, and make sure there is nothing left undone for tomorrow that might be important to you. Argue with your mother on the phone today? Call her that night, and go to sleep as friends—never with unfinished business that has to wait for a day that may never arrive.

So many people waste the time of their lives. Sitting in front of television is a waste of your mind. Getting so out of shape you can't participate in life is a waste of that life. Not reading and enjoying the endless works of people who want to share stories, lives, and adventures is a waste of your life. What "Nothing lasts forever" really means is that you have to live your life—now, today, and every day until it is taken away from you.

1. Nothing lasts forever. What does this mean to you in your life?

2. Getting the most out of each day is one of the hard lessons in life? Do you live each day seeking the most you can get or do you waste the days of your life?

3. What are the biggest time-wasters in your life? Why are you willing to waste something so precious as your life with these things?

4. If you only had one more day to live, how would you live it? Who would you spend it with? What would you do?

5. Life for many ends too soon. What are you doing now to live a full and rich life that will have meaning and make a difference?

6. What if you weren't there for your children? Write a secret letter, and lock it away for them in case you aren't always there to tell them about who you are and how you feel about them.

Your life, your family

Always remember
Papa loves you

One final letter, my child,

There would be nothing sweeter to contemplate in my life than to dream of walking on a beach with you, or through a mountain meadow, when you are 21. The thought of spending hours with you as an adult, talking about all things important and all that is beautiful in life, would be a definitive statement for me, summing up a part of my life that would then be more complete.

The dream is there in my aging head, but the man is here now, and it is impossible to know if I will be there in your future, and even if I am, will I be able to share everything then that means so much to me now? Life and the heavens have their own agendas, and the best we can do is to try to live as well as we can now and let life as we know it take its own course.

Perhaps the hardest part of this book is letting you know who I am now as I write this for you. This has to be the dream of every grandparent who stands before an older grandchild as a tired, mostly bald old man in funny clothes or a woman of indeterminable shape in baggy high-waist pants and white athletic shoes screaming inside his or her head that this is not who I really am and is definitely not who I was when I lived a younger person's life. Even those who spend much of their lives taking care of themselves can still stand with their grandchildren and wish that for just a few minutes they could show them who they used to be before age changed the reflection in the mirror forever.

We all used to be somebody. We were young, had adventures, went to school, started a career, had children, and lived a full and active life, but to the grandchildren, we are the old guys who drive badly, sleep in the big chair during the holidays, and tell endless stories of our youth. You might remember a few moments with us from when you were small that somehow became etched in your brain as a little girl, but it is a shame that these few moments become all that is left of us as you age. Who we are now, my sweet girl, is not who we were, but helping you understand that is immensely hard.

This book was written so you would remember everyone in your life as people who lived and loved you as a child and who will remember you forever and a minute. I hope that everyone who reads this book will use it to leave a story of his or her own life and that what he or she believes and who he or she is is not lost to his or her grandchildren and even his or her children.

Letting grandchildren know who their grandparents were when the grandparents were young, vital, and part of life seems so easy in theory, but in reality is so hard to accomplish. Looking at a few old photos on the computer, or even ones that exist from the days of your grandparents' youth that now gather dust in an album pulled out of the closet every decade or so, reduces a person to nothing more than shadows that become more and more faded in memory each year.

Writing this book took several years, and most of it was written on planes as I traveled around the world, giving workshops and trying to help people grow and prosper. This for me is the place to start my brief tale because what I did for work is what eventually defined most of my adult life and eventually led to this book. The details of what I did and where I lived are there for you to find, but who I was as an adult is much more important to the story being told here, and that is what I will try to write for you.

There was a popular craze traveling around the country when this book was written that centered on using software to find our details about family members that seem to be lost in the family lore. This was always a flawed way to view someone in my opinion. Knowing where you lived, or the company you worked for, tells someone where that person spent time, and perhaps that is important to some people, but the real story is who was that person, what did they believe, and how did they choose to work and live their lives. Grandparents should pass through more of what they thought and how they approached the big lessons in life rather than just raw dates and details that can't define the person in any way.

My life always seemed to be a mismatch of career choices that were never quite connected, but the sum of everything I did gave me a great advantage through the years because the total of my life's experiences always gave me a way to help the person in front of me. So many people start on one course, change direction, and believe that they are on a totally different path, but in actuality, they are just gaining tools and maturity to accomplish the big mission that isn't always revealed early in life. We become who we are through the accumulation of experiences in life, and through the decisions we made up to last night, and the combination of those components should always lead us closer toward realizing our passions and big dreams.

In college, I studied psychology and journalism, which seemed an odd combination at the time, but learning about how people think and learning how to write turned out to be the most important decisions I made at a young age. These two seemingly disconnected choices became the foundation for most of what I did from that point forward as a consultant, which always sounds somewhat nebulous when someone asks what you do for a living, but is really nothing more than helping people solve problems they can't seem to solve themselves.

The third pillar of my life was fitness, which eventually became the source of everything else. Sports were a part of my life through school, and while I wasn't a gifted athlete in any sense, taking care of myself physically became a lifelong fascination and obsession. Going to graduate school meant the need for money, and the best opportunity at the time was working in a local gym, and except for about six months working as a schoolteacher, I never worked again outside of the fitness industry.

All the steps on this convoluted path evolved into becoming a business specialist who worked almost exclusively with fitness businesses. There were always other opportunities in other fields that often presented themselves and that I accepted for the challenge of learning something new, but my passion for fitness and the people who dedicated their lives in this industry to helping others kept me returning to this group of passionate believers.

Someone once asked me, "What do you actually do for a living?" It seemed that I always had too much fun working and that from the outside, it never appeared that what I chose to do to support myself looked like work. It took me more than 30 years to get the maturity to answer this question, but finally, I was able to say when asked: "I exist to change lives. It is what I do, and it is what I get paid for in my life."

If there was anything I would want you to remember about me forever, my perfect child, is that I cared deeply about helping others become the best they could be in their lives, which is probably why I wrote this book for a child of six who might not understand much of it for another 15 to 20 years.

Your life should have meaning, and when you are gone, what you did should have meant something. People aren't remembered for making money; they are remembered for what they did with the money while they were here. Most importantly, people are remembered for the lives they touched and the others they helped through their short journey on this planet.

There was also an old saying that was used often during the earlier parts of my life, and that defined who I was and how I thought. This simple phrase made for a good life, and perhaps got me into a little trouble now and then too—but trouble worth the effort if it meant leading an interesting life.

The words in this phrase rang simple and clear in my mind, but also resonated with a deep meaning to me: Life is lived on the edge. Mediocrity is the cautious side of life, and people who live on the edge of life are the ones who live life as it was meant to be. The best days of your life, such as when your granddaughter was born, are not days you remember as safe or moderate, but days when everything in life is good and special. The best day in your career, the best day of vacation ever, the best day when you find someone to love could never be defined as moderate days—they are remembered for the rest of your life as days that momentarily took you away from the simple and the average to the special and the remembered.

Never do anything where you are not all in and committed. If you want to be a friend, pick your friends carefully and then be the best friend ever. If you go to school or pick a career, work to be the best that ever was, not just another mediocre participant in a job that goes nowhere and where your days are filled with dreams of being somewhere else. Whatever you do, take it to the edge, and seek the total experience or commitment, and never enter into anything where you are not fully willing to appreciate the time spent because trading your life one day at a time is how life is truly defined.

There was also a part of me that was never completely satisfied when I was young. There were always adventures to be had and places to move and try. There was just too much life and not enough me, and I wanted it all as quickly as I could find it.

Nana and your mother finally provided the anchors that allowed me to slow down and appreciate life at a different pace. Being part of a family, even when you are almost 50 when you get it started, was a settling influence, but it took years of trying the world on for size before I was able to fully appreciate what I had found.

It is hard to describe through short pages written to someone who will be you in the future, but maybe the true secret of life is being able to chase your passion and yet stay anchored to something that is bigger. My life was always out there somewhere else, teaching people how to make money and to live fuller lives, but one still needs a family that understands that need to keep going and chasing my dream.

There don't seem to be many people who ultimately find their passion, let alone dedicate their lives to living their own dreams, and that is a sad part of life and the sad part of trying to help others. This is also why so many people live lives of an ever-increasing frustration as they age, knowing that with each birthday, their dreams are slipping further and further away.

So, who was your Papa, my perfect child, and what will you remember of him? Remember me as a man who found love and family late in life, but who found that these are perhaps the greatest gifts of life. Remember me as someone who cared and took it personally if I tried to help you and you failed to live up to the talent you possessed. Wasting your life and your talent is the biggest sin in life and something I never tolerated well with those I believed in.

Also, remember me as someone who created a life that could be lived on my own terms. Life is something taken for granted by the dull of mind, wasted by the fools who believe tomorrow will never come, and over too soon for those who don't value their own health and well-being. Life can also be rich, full, and deep for those who are willing to think about the power of the gift and who work hard every single day to master the tools of life enhancement.

But if you remember nothing else about me, my child, remember this: Your Papa, a man who found love difficult and found it late in life, loved you with all the love a grandparent can summon. This book was supposed to be about future gifts for you, but perhaps it is really a book about what the love of your Nana, your mother, and you gave to me.

Remember, Madison, and remember it always on those days you feel alone: Papa always loved you and always will.

1. How do you want to be remembered by your children? Write a letter, or your own book, and leave a legacy of words and pictures as to who you are, what you believed, and how you lived, including all the stories and wisdom you would want to pass to your children.

2. Don't miss the opportunity to share your life with others. Somewhere in the future will be someone who wants to know about you and who you were. Create letters and stories now that can be shared by a generation in the future.

Your life, your family

Your life, your family

About the Author

Hansen Photography

Thomas Plummer has been a business consultant specializing in the fitness industry for over 35 years and has been recognized as one of the most influential people to ever work in the industry due to the popularity of his workshops around the world and his bestselling books. While he has written seven books on the business of fitness, this is his first book on the lessons of life. Most of his 35 years in the fitness business were spent coaching young people who were trying to live their dream of making a difference in their world by working in an industry that can create change in so many people's lives. The lessons learned from these passionate and dedicated young fitness professionals, and the ideas that were shared with so many in exchange, gave birth to this book. There are many questions in life and many people seeking direction. This book was written to help people find their own path and to help people live a life that is fulfilled and meaningful. Thomas currently lives in Florida and, as always, is working on the next book.

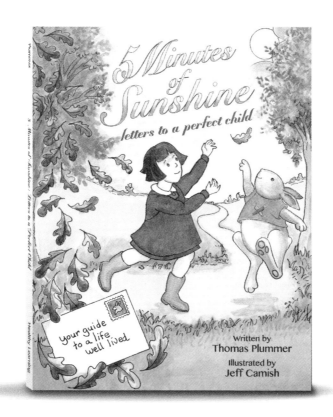

5 Minutes of Sunshine
Letters to a Perfect Child

By Thomas Plummer

Available at HealthyLearning.com